The Thucydides Trap And US-China Rivalry: Lessons From History

GEW Intelligence Unit

Global East-West. London

Copyright © 2025 by GEW Intelligence Unit

Essays, Reports and Analyses: A Global East-West Series

Edited by Hichem Karoui.

All rights reserved. No part of this book may be reproduced in any manner whatsoever without written permission, except for brief quotations incorporated into critical articles and reviews.

First printing, 2025.

Contents

1. Preface: Literature Review — 1
   by Hichem Karoui
2. Introduction — 23
   Understanding the Thucydides Trap
3. Historical Precedents — 41
   Lessons from the Peloponnesian War
4. Rivalry and Cooperation — 59
   The Anglo-German Naval Arms Race
5. Transitions of Power — 77
   The US-UK Example Post-WWII
6. A Contemporary Analysis — 97
   The Rise of China
7. Economic Competitions — 117
   Trade and Technological Supremacy
8. Military Dynamics and Security Concerns — 139
9. Policy Choices — 157
   Steering Away from Conflict

10. Global Challenges   177
    Opportunities for US-China Cooperation

11. Future Scenarios   197
    Navigating the Path Ahead

Selected Bibliography   215

1

Preface: Literature Review
by Hichem Karoui

I. Introduction

The notion of the "Thucydides Trap," a concept that has gained prominence through the work of American political scientist Graham T. Allison, is a crucial analytical lens. It helps us understand the increasing likelihood of conflict when a rising power challenges an existing great power. This concept, inspired by the Athenian historian Thucydides' reflection on the Peloponnesian War, is not just a historical pattern but a warning sign. Thucydides famously proclaimed that "it was the rise of Athens and the fear that this instilled in Sparta that made war inevitable." The growing acceptance of this concept, especially in the context of the United States and China relations, is a stark reminder of the urgent need to address the potential conflict. The contention between the United States as today's global hegemon and China as the rapidly emerging power poses and will continue to pose, arguably the most significant and dangerous threat in international relations. Studying historical context and possible conflict situations in such frameworks is thus crucial. This review set out to collect, analyse, and evaluate the existing scholarly works focused on the "Thucydides Trap" in the scope of US-China relations.

The present Essay is designed to achieve several objectives: propose strategies to mitigate conflict between the United States and China, evaluate historical case studies of power shifts, discuss critiques and alternative perspectives, analyse arguments for and against the relevance of the Thucydides Trap in the modern context, and explore the contemporary significance of this concept.

II. Understanding The Thucydides Trap

The 'Thucydides Trap concept became widely known through Graham Allison's work at Harvard, especially in his book, 'Destined for War.' In this book, he explains that the 'Thucydides Trap' means the unfortunate position a rising nation faces when trying to challenge an already established power because, in the past, this has resulted in war. He believes that the United States and China are in this particular situation together because China becoming stronger is challenging the United States' position as a superpower. The main idea of the 'Thucydides Trap' has to do with 'structural stress', which refers to the inflexion point of competition and conflict that emerges when a rising nation threatens to take over a ruling nation, making war far more possible. This was directly taken from Thucydides' narration of the Peloponnesian War, where he said its outbreak was bound to happen for all reasons if Athenian power grew and the Spartans were fearful.

He tried to prove his hypothesis by analysing 16 documented case studies of the power-balance shift. His analysis concluded that in 12 of these 16 cases, the power transition resulted in war between the two powers. These results suggest a considerable link between the powerful shifts and the conflict, supporting the argument of a "trap" for these states.

While Allison argues from a clear quantitative perspective using the information provided in the study, it is worth noting that the specific historical examples selected are often contested along with the reasoning given for their interpretation. The context of the Peloponnesian War, which is originally the source for this phrase, was a multi-causal problem not merely the prime ascent of Athenian and Spartan fear. These also included the rivalry between alliance systems, certain provocative incidents, and the decisions made by leaders in various other city-states. Regardless of the "deterministic" feel of the "Thucydides Trap," no less important is the fact that the war, as stressed by Allison, is not predetermined. Rather, the strife on balance created by a power on the rise and a dominant power in control greatly increases conflict. It is without doubt that in most cases significant diplomatic action is needed most of the time to defuse a situation poised to explode. This underscores the crucial role of diplomacy in preventing potential conflicts.

III. The Thucydides Trap and US-China Rivalry: An Overview of the Literature

The application of 'Thucydides Trap' on the United States and China relations has become a mainstay in academic and policy debates. The term became popular after 2015 when it started being used broadly to explain the relations of competition and cooperation between the two powers. Critical scholars like Graham Allison, for example, have studied this application thoroughly, contending that China's growth and challenge to the US-dominated global order resonates with the historical narrative of Thucydides Trap. Other prominent international relations figures, John Mearsheimer, without using the term 'Thucydides Trap,' have likewise cautioned against the emerging conflict from the power shift of the US and China, adopting a realist stance, one that focuses on great power rivalry as a dominant force in this world.

The notion has also spread beyond academia into

the political and media commentary spaces in both the US and China. Chinese President Xi Jinping has publicly warned about falling into a Thucydides Trap while, at other times, denying its inevitability, indicating an awareness at the highest levels of leadership of the dangers posed by the ongoing transition of power.

That this concept, rooted in the distant past and made famous by an American academic, is being talked about by Chinese leaders showcases how deeply this concept is embedded into the complexities of the bilateral relations between the two countries. However, the fact that some interpretations, like that which uses a more combative approach towards China, and the deliberate manipulation of the phrase in the US political discourse, indicates a more sophisticated approach is essential when trying to understand the concept within the context of US-China relations. This complexity underscores the need for a nuanced and comprehensive understanding of the Thucydides Trap and its implications for US-China relations.

IV. Arguments for the Applicability of the Thucydides Trap to the US-China Rivalry

Several arguments within the academic literature support the applicability and relevance of the "Thucydides Trap" to the current dynamic between the United States and China. A primary focus lies on the structural factors inherent in the relationship, particularly the dramatic rise of China's economic, military, and technological power over the past few decades. This unprecedented ascent has positioned China as a direct challenger to the established hegemony of the United States in the international system. Across various dimensions, from economic output and technological innovation to military modernisation and global influence, China is increasingly seen as a peer competitor to the United States. Many analysts argue that this fundamental shift in the balance of power creates the structural stress that Allison identifies as the core of the "Thucydides Trap".

This rapid and comprehensive rise of China often mirrors the historical conditions that led to conflict in Allison's case studies. The metrics used to assess China's growth, such as its increasing share of global GDP, advancements in key technologies, and expanding military capabilities, are frequently cited as evidence of a power transition that inevitably challenges the existing order. Consequently, the established power, the United States, may experience inherent fear and insecurity in response to China's growing strength and influence. Just as Sparta feared the rise of Athens, some scholars argue that the United States perceives China's ascent as a potential threat to its global standing, security interests, and the liberal international order it has long championed. This fear can manifest in various ways, including increased military spending, forming alliances to contain China's influence, and a more assertive foreign policy in regions where US and Chinese interests intersect.

Furthermore, the literature highlights specific tension and potential flashpoints in the US-China relationship that could escalate within the "Thucydides Trap" framework. Taiwan's continued de facto independence, supported by the United States, is a major point of contention, with China viewing the island as a renegade province that must eventually be reunified with the mainland. China's assertive actions and territorial claims in the South China Sea, including its island-building campaign and restrictions on international access, also fuel regional tensions and raise concerns about potential military confrontation. Economic issues, such as trade imbalances, intellectual property theft, and technological competition, further contribute to the rivalry. Finally, fundamental ideological differences between the democratic values of the United States and the authoritarian system in China create a deeper layer of mistrust and suspicion, potentially exacerbating the security dilemma. These specific areas of friction provide tangible examples of how the broader structural competition between a rising and a ruling power could manifest in ways that increase the risk of conflict.

V. Historical Lessons: Rising Powers and Established Powers

The academic literature frequently examines historical cases of rising powers challenging established powers to draw lessons relevant to the current US-China dynamic.

Graham Allison's study of 16 such instances provides a starting point, with cases like the conflict between France and the Habsburgs in the 16th century, the rivalry between Great Britain and France in the 18th and 19th centuries, and the rise of Germany challenging the United Kingdom in the early 20th century often cited as examples where power transitions led to war.

#	Period	Ruling Power	Rising Power	Result	Key Lessons/Relevance to US-China
1	Late 15th century	Portugal	Spain	No war	Power transition managed peacefully; potential for negotiated settlements.
2	First half of 16th century	France	Habsburgs	War	Competition for European dominance led to prolonged conflict.
3	16th and 17th centuries	Habsburgs	Ottoman Empire	War	Clash of empires with differing ideologies and territorial ambitions.
4	First half of 17th century	Habsburgs	Sweden	War	Religious and political tensions exacerbated by power shift.
5	Mid-to-late 17th century	Dutch Republic	England	War	Commercial rivalry and naval competition led to conflict.
6	Late 17th to mid-18th centuries	France	Great Britain	War	Protracted struggle for global dominance.
7	Late 18th and early 19th centuries	United Kingdom	France	War	Revolutionary ideology and hegemonic ambitions clashed.
8	Mid-19th century	France and United Kingdom	Russia	War	Competition over influence in the Ottoman Empire.
9	Mid-19th century	France	Germany	War	Rise of German nationalism and military power altered European balance
10	Late 19th and early 20th centuries	China and Russia	Japan	War	Emerging Japan challenged declining regional powers.
11	Early 20th century	United Kingdom	United States	No war	Peaceful transition; accommodation of rising power's interests.
12	Early 20th century	United Kingdom (supported by France, Russia)	Germany	War	Complex factors including alliance systems and nationalism.
13	Mid-20th century	Soviet Union, France, and United Kingdom	Germany	War	Aggressive expansionism of rising power.
14	Mid-20th century	United States	Japan	War	Clash of imperial ambitions in the Pacific.
15	1940s-1980s	United States	Soviet Union	Cold (proxy) war / economic/trade war	Intense rivalry avoided direct war through deterrence and diplomacy.
16	1990s-present	United Kingdom and France	Germany	Cold (proxy) war / economic/trade war	Economic competition within a framework of cooperation.

In the lead-up to World War I, the Anglo-German naval race provides another relevant historical parallel.

The desire of Germany to create a fleet to rival Britain's Royal Navy – the foremost naval power during that period – set off an aggressive arms race within Europe and significantly strained relations between the two countries. Although this rivalry didn't directly initiate the war in 1914, it created a relationship of distrust and animosity that complicated peaceful negotiations. This historical example illustrates how aggressive consolidation of military resources by a challenger power intent on displacing a dominant global influence can strain relations and foster conditions conducive to warfare.

On the other hand, the Cold War period of rivalry between the United States and the Soviet Union is an example of a conflict between two superpowers that, despite their sharp ideological divides and perilous arms race, never resulted in direct warfare. The policy of mutually assured destruction, which stated that neither side would initiate a nuclear strike because both would incur disastrous consequences, prevented direct assaults. Moreover, other arms control treaties, setting up relations to reduce tension, and active diplomacy effectively mitigated the risk of conflict.

The Cold War analysis not only indicates the manageability of high tensions between superpowers without leading to warfare but also highlights the significant role of diplomacy and deterrence in preserving peace. The literature on the Peloponnesian War offers insights into the fear of great power conflicts and the dangers of an alliance arms race and mutual destruction, instilling hope for conflict resolution.

VI. Critiques and Other Views on the Context of Thucydides Trap in US-China Relations

The 'Thucydides Trap' as a thesis has garnered criticism due to its popularity as well as its influences, especially in the case of China and the US. The trap, a term coined by political scientist Graham Allison, refers to the likelihood of conflict when a rising power challenges a ruling power. The critics of the prevailing methodology employed by Allison in his study claim to have issues with the chosen approach, along with the interpretation of historical examples. A section of historians believes that Allison misattributed the analyses of conflicts in consideration. For example, some scholars contend that the underlying unifying force of a power transition thesis misses out on much deeper causal reasons for conflict. In their case, World War I is cited as an outcome of complex alliance systems, rampant nationalism, and miscalculations from numerous leaders that contended, albeit not solely, but due to German ascendance and Britain's eclipse.

Also, some of Allison's definitions for "rising power" and "ruling power" in some of the cases have been challenged. Allison's focus on structural factors receives criticism for lacking the human agency and the leadership strategies decided by the actors involved.

Aside from the methodological controversies, a broader debate exists about the precedents set by history that the US-China context uses; these differences are argued to be much more distinct than previous examples. The sheer degree of economic interdependence that exists between the United States and China today is often used as a major counterargument. Their economies are so integrated through trade, investment, and global supply chains that a major conflict between the two countries is likely to incur massive costs for both, presenting a strong deterrence. Both having nuclear arsenals also changes the pose for conflict, as the risk of mutually assured destruction fundamentally shifts the rationale for conflict. Most of the historical examples provided by

Allison did not have this case. The contemporary form of globalisation, with its intricate information, finance, and people networks, marks a distinct difference from earlier periods of great power competition. Beyond the "Thucydides Trap," the exploration of broader suggestions offers an engaging understanding of US-China relations within alternative theoretical frameworks. In a different scope, power transition theory covers the relations between rising and declining states and their conflict expectations with differing violent outcomes, inviting the audience to explore different perspectives.

The 'Kindleberger Trap' concludes that the menace lies not in China, which is too powerful, but in America, as a declining hegemon that does not offer sufficient public goods to the system. This theory, proposed by Charles Kindleberger, suggests that when a dominant power fails to provide public goods, such as economic stability and security, a power vacuum is created, leading to conflict. 'Silver Way' offers a different historical paradigm by looking at the 16th and 17th centuries, where trade with an emerging Spain and a powerful China saw economic integration without significant violent conflict. Lastly, some postulate that it is more productive to analyse the US-China relationship through the focus on the interplay of status competition instead of just material power balance, paying attention to how deeply important recognition and esteem are for both nations.

VII. Strategies and Solutions for Preventing the Thucydides Trap

The analysis of the Thucydides Trap about the US-China rivalry also seeks to formulate multiple conflict avoidance strategies. As tension mitigation and enhancing understanding are vital goals, some propose multi-tier diplomatic interactions as a primary device for engagement. Keeping several lines of communication open, even if contentious, helps curtail escalation as intentions can be properly conveyed and used to diminish unintended consequences.

International collaboration regarding issues in a global context where the interests of both the US and China align presents another best strategy. Transnational problems such as climate change, global pandemics, and sustaining economies bolster competition and foster collaboration, which establishes a trust base to manage competition in other areas. "Peaceful competition" purports that the rivalry between the two nations does not equate to the conflict that will inevitably happen but rather a conflict that can be tamed within the norms set by both the US and China. Some scholars argue more about the need for the United States to exercise an emerging restive foreign policy that aims for counterbalancing forces instead of dominating powers, suggesting the heuristics of this policy would lead the US to grant more agency to allies while concentrating on core strategic interests, along with reducing the primary influence in international relations. This stance may lower the security dilemma it faces with China.

Both sides also valued identifying common weaknesses and adjusting to China's rise. As explained in the book Avoiding "The Thucydides Trap": U.S.-China Relation in Strategic Domains, considerable tension exists in maritime security and nuclear stability, cyberspace, and space, which warrants managing the relationship through collaboration rather than confrontation.

VIII. Conclusion

Discussion of The Thucydides Trap suggests a fundamental conflict of interest poised to erupt when an emergent rival faces an already established power. This literature review has focused on its prospects concerning the competition between the United States and China. In the U.S.-China debate, one finds Graham Allison's definition useful: There is a dangerous dynamic about the Trap, and its proof lies in analysing the centre of structural stress during transitions of power—arguably one of the most contentious perspectives on US relations with China. The literature illustrates an alarming volume of work interpreting the concept within these boundaries, especially drawing attention to the growing economic prowess of China alongside the increasing fear and insecurity it poses to the United States, encapsulating the essence of the Trap dynamic.

At the same time, the review notes major criticisms of the "Thucydides Trap," such as pointing out the inconsistencies of Allison's historical reasoning and the striking differences between the existing US-China relations and history. It is often noted that factors such as the profound economic integration of the states and the existence of nuclear arms serve to change the present dynamics. Other theoretical approaches, including more softened versions of the power transition theory, the "Kindleberger Trap," the "Silver Way," and those that centre on competition for status, provide alternative insights into the intricate struggle and interactions.

Notwithstanding the controversy regarding its relevance, "Thucydides Trap" is a useful heuristic about the dangers of great power competition. It is clear from the literature that there are several ways to avert conflict, many of which share the necessity of diplomacy, international collaboration on common issues, self-restraint, and prioritising mutual benefits. In any case, although history can provide some contours, the leaders of the United States and China will determine, through their strategies, the relations between the two countries. A careful analysis of the history, the present, and the existing academic debate is essential to study this policy area.

References

Allison, G. T. (2017). *Destined for war: Can America and China escape Thucydides's trap?* Houghton Mifflin Harcourt.

Bönker, D. (2015). Naval Race between Germany and Great Britain 1898-1912. In *International Encyclopedia of the First World War*.

Copeland, D. (n.d.). *economic interdependence and the future of u.s.-chinese relations*.

CSIS. (2024). *Advancing U.S.-China Coordination Amid Strategic Competition: An Emerging Playbook*. Retrieved from https://www.csis.org/analysis/advancing-us-china-coordination-amid-strategic-competition-emerging-playbook

CSIS. (2024). *U.S.-China Relations in 2024: Managing Competition Without Conflict*. Retrieved from https://www.csis.org/analysis/us-china-relations-2024-managing-competition-without-conflict

Desch, M. C. (2025). Balancing Away from War: How the USA and China Can Side-step the Thucydides' Trap. *The Chinese Journal of International Politics*, 18(2), 151–172.

EADaily. (2024, December 30). John Mearsheimer: It makes no sense for the United States to fight with Russia, but with by China. *EADaily*. Retrieved from https://eadaily.com/en/news/2024/12/30/john-mearsheimer-it-makes-no-sense-for-the-united-states-to-fight-with-russia-but-with-by-china

Fallows, J. (2017, March 6). The United States, China, and the Thucydides Trap. *The Fletcher Forum of World Affairs*. Retrieved from https://www.fletcherforum.org/home/2017/3/6/the-united-states-china-and-the-thucydides-trap

Geopolitical Futures. (2020, July 8). The Thucydides Trap and the Rise and Fall of Great Powers. *Geopolitical Futures*. Retrieved from https://geopoliticalfutures.com/the-thucydides-trap-and-the-rise-and-fall-of-great-powers/

Gordon, P., & Morales, J. J. (2017, June 19). The 'Silver Way': An Alternative to 'Thucydides Trap' – The Diplomat. *The Diplomat*. Retrieved from https://thediplomat.com/2017/06/the-silver-way-an-alternative-to-thucydides-trap/

Harvard Kennedy School. (n.d.). *Destined for War: Can America and China Escape Thucydides's Trap?* Retrieved from https://www.hks.harvard.edu/publications/destined-war-can-america-and-china-escape-thucydidess-trap

Harvard University. (n.d.). *Discussing Thucydides Trap*. Retrieved from https://gsas.harvard.edu/news/discussing-thucydides-trap

Institute for National Strategic Studies. (2019). *Thucydides's Other Traps? The United States, China, and the Prospect of Inevitable War*.

IWM. (n.d.). *The Naval Race Between Britain And Germany Before The First World War*. Retrieved from https://www.iwm.org.uk/history/the-naval-race-between-britain-and-germany-before-the-first-world-war

Jervis, R. (1991). The Future of World Politics: Will It Resemble the Past? *International Security, 16*(3), 39–73.

Kagan, D. (1995). *Thucydides: The Reinvention of History*. Penguin Books.

Kamphausen, R. D., Drun, J., Hui, X., Ying, Y., Colby, E. A., Riqiang, W., Segal, A., Lan, T., Weeden, B.,

He, X., Tanner, T., & Minghao, Z. (2022). *Avoiding the "Thucydides Trap": U.S.-China Relations in Strategic Domains*. Routledge.

Lebow, R. N. (1994). The Long Peace, the End of the Cold War, and the Failure of Realism. *International Organization, 48*(2), 249–277.

Liping, X. (2021). *Nuclear Disarmament*.

Lobell, S. E. (2021). Can the United States and China Escape the Thucydides Trap? *China International Strategy Review, 3*(1), 81–98.

Maoz, Z. (1993). *The Causes of International Conflict: From Classical Realism to the Democratic Peace*. Westview Press.

Mazarr, M. J., et al. (2018). *Understanding the Emerging Era of International Competition*. RAND Corporation.

McKinney, J. (2015). *Structure and Contingency: The Causes of the Peloponnesian War*.

Mearsheimer, J. J. (1990). Back to the Future: Instability in Europe After the Cold War. *International Security, 15*(1), 5–56.

Mearsheimer, J. J. (2001). *The tragedy of great power politics*. W. W. Norton & Company.

Mearsheimer, J. J. (2024). Reflections on John Mearsheimer's China Trip: Popularity, Influence, and Implications. *The Chinese Journal of International Politics, 18*(3), 387–402.

Misenheimer, A. G. (2018). *Thucydides's Other Traps? The United States, China, and the Prospect of Inevitable War*.

Mukherjee, R. (2020). *Ascending Order: Rising Powers and the Politics of Status in International Institutions*. Cambridge University Press.

National Museum of World War II. (n.d.). *Cold Conflict.* Retrieved from https://www.nationalww2museum.org/war/articles/cold-conflict

NDISC. (2023, January 19). To Set and Spring the Thucydides Trap. *NDISC.* Retrieved from https://ndisc.nd.edu/news-media/news/to-set-and-spring-the-thucydides-trap/

Nye, J. S. (2017). Trump and the Kindleberger Trap. *Project Syndicate.*

Nye, J.S. (2023). The Kindleberger Trap. In: Soft Power and Great-Power Competition. China and Globalization. Springer, Singapore. https://doi.org/10.1007/978-981-99-0714-4_26

Nye, J. S. (2023, October 26). Lecture | Joseph Nye: The U.S. and China are NOT destined for war. *Peking University.* Retrieved from http://newsen.pku.edu.cn/news_events/news/global/13719.html

Organski, A. F. K. (1958). *World Politics.* Alfred A. Knopf.

Perseus Digital Library. (n.d.). Thucydides, The History of the Peloponnesian War, Book 1, chapter 12, section 1, subsection 2. *Perseus Tufts.* Retrieved from https://www.perseus.tufts.edu/hopper/text?doc=Perseus%3Atext%3A1999.04.0009%3Achapter%3D12%3Asection%3D1%3Asubsection%3D2

Pillsbury, M. (2015). *The Hundred-Year Marathon: China's Secret Strategy to Replace America as the Global Superpower.* Henry Holt and Company.

RAND Corporation. (2018). *Understanding the Emerging Era of International Competition.*

Rosecrance, R. (1986). The Rise of the Trading State: Commerce and Conquest in the Modern World. *Basic Books.*

Rudd, K. (2023). *The Avoidable War: The Dangers of a Catastrophic Conflict Between the US and Xi Jinping's China.* PublicAffairs.

Scanlon, T. F. (2002). *Eros and Greek Athletics.* Oxford University Press.

Schwarz, B., & Layne, C. (1999). A Dangerous Unipolar World. *International Security, 24*(2), 114–141.

Singer, J. D., & Wildavsky, A. B. (1993). *The Real World Order: Zones of Peace, Zones of Turmoil.* Chatham House Publishers.

Singer, J. D., Bremer, S., & Stuckey, J. (1972). Capability Distribution, Uncertainty, and Major Power War, 1820-1965. In *Peace, War, and Numbers* (pp. 19–48). Sage Publications, Inc.

Siverson, R. M., & Sullivan, M. P. (1983). The Distribution of Power and the Onset of War. *The Journal of Conflict Resolution, 27*(3), 473–494.

Siverson, R. M., & Tennefoss, R. (1984). Power, Alliance, and the Onset of War. *American Journal of Political Science, 28*(2), 275–295.

State.gov. (n.d.). *U.S. Relations With China.* Retrieved from https://www.state.gov/u-s-relations-with-china/

Sullivan, D. (2018, January 24). Destined for Competition: An Analysis of Graham Allison's Thucydides Trap. *The Strategy Bridge.* Retrieved from https://thestrategybridge.org/the-bridge/2018/1/24/destined-for-competition-an-analysis-of-graham-allisons-thucydides-trap

Tanner, T. N., & Wang, D. (Eds.). (2020). *Avoiding the "Thucydides Trap": U.S.-China Relations in Strategic Domains.* Routledge.

Thucydides. (n.d.). *History of the Peloponnesian War.*

United States Department of State. (n.d.). *Cold War Diplomacy, 1945-1991.* Retrieved from https://diplomacy.state.gov/discover-diplomacy/period/cold-war-diplomacy/

University of Notre Dame. (2023, January 19). To Set and Spring the Thucydides Trap. *NDISC.* Retrieved from https://ndisc.nd.edu/news-media/news/to-set-and-spring-the-thucydides-trap/

Wang, Y. (2023). Understanding the Current China-US Relationship through the "Thucydides Trap." *Journal of Student Research, 12*(3).

Xia Liping. (2021). *Nuclear Disarmament.*

Xinhua News Agency. (2024, October 19). Full text of John Mearsheimer's interview with Global Times: Security competition between China and the US is inevitable, but the war can be prevented - Global Times. *Global Times.* Retrieved from https://www.globaltimes.cn/page/202410/1322018.shtml

Yoshihara, T. (n.d.). *China's Rise and Maritime Commons Dilemmas.*

Zhiqun Zhu. (2024, September 5). Understanding China's Perceptions and Strategy Toward Nuclear Weapons: A Case Study Approach. *Asia Society.* Retrieved from https://asiasociety.org/policy-institute/understanding-chinas-perceptions-and-strategy-toward-nuclear-weapons-case-study-approach

Zhu, Z. (2024, July 17). Political Drivers of China's Changing Nuclear Policy: Implications for U.S.-China Nuclear Relations and International Security. *Carnegie Endowment for International Peace*. Retrieved from https://carnegieendowment.org/research/2024/07/china-nuclear-buildup-political-drivers-united-states-relationship-international-security

Zhu, Z. (2024, October 17). US-China Relations for the 2030s: Toward a Realistic Scenario for Coexistence. *Carnegie Endowment for International Peace*. Retrieved from https://carnegieendowment.org/research/2024/10/us-china-relations-for-the-2030s-toward-a-realistic-scenario-for-coexistence

2

Introduction
Understanding the Thucydides Trap

Contextualising the Thucydides Trap

The Thucydides Trap, a term first used by political scientist Graham T. Allison, describes the conflict that is bound to arise from competition between an emerging power and a preexisting power, akin to the Greek historian Thucydides' description of the Peloponnesian War. This idea has received considerable focus in modern international relations because of its direct relevance to the analysis of superpowers that emerge to challenge global hegemons. Understanding how this notion pertains to contemporary international friction and its applicability across multiple historical periods is crucial for grasping the implications of opportunity and risk associated with power shifts on the world stage. The changing landscape of modern geopolitics necessitates both empirical and theoretical frameworks on the Thucydides Trap. It is applied to issues such as the rise of China against the backdrop of the United States' superpower status as well as other historical power contests including the Anglo-German naval arms race that subsequently resulted in the two world wars. Such incidents highlight the value of studying different historical eras marked by conflicts that were fuelled by changing power relations.

In its economic, ideological, and military forms of competition, the Thucydides Trap encapsulates the vulnerabilities that powers shifting in a global hierarchy bring. It is useful today for discussions regarding the implications of China's rise in power relative to the existing global order. To explain the Thucydides Trap, one must address the intersection of international relations and history during the upheaval of the power structure, looking to different historical periods to make sense of the intricacies of international relations and the balance of power. After these examinations, it becomes evident how Grady's insights explain the coherence of the Thucydides Trap across multiple contexts.

Defining the Concept: Empirical and Theoretical Perspectives

The concept of the Thucydides Trap has not only piqued the interest of diplomatic circles and policy discourse but also attracted scholarly attention. It focuses on the rivalry and challenges related to power between a rising challenger and an established incumbent on the international stage. While the term can be traced back to Thucydides' documentation of the Peloponnesian War, its complexity is more relevant to modern geopolitical changes, particularly the increasing conflict between the USA and China. The scholarly focus has extended to presenting case studies of the geopolitics of Europe in the 19th century and the strategic relations of other regions in the world to demonstrate the dynamics of the Thucydides Trap. Moreover, the concept of the Thucydides Trap has been developed not only in terms of historical analogies but also from theories based on other fields like political science, economics, and sociology. This interdisciplinary approach allows for the study of the intricate relationships that result from power shifts, global stability, and the factors influencing them.

Additionally, the diverse range of interpretations that integrate realists to consider power-centric state relations and constructivists' focus on identity perception and international relations underscores the concept's profound attention within academia. To further add to the concept's understanding, the incorporation of game theory and decision theory provides models that analyse the rational calculations and strategic decisions of actors involved in the Thucydides Trap. We seek to build a foundational understanding of the empirical and theoretical evidence surrounding the Thucydides Trap and its effects on contemporary politics and international relations.

Historical background and origins

The origins and historical background of the Thucydides Trap are deeply rooted in the ancient Greek historian Thucydides' writings, especially regarding the Peloponnesian War. The account by Thucydides contains important lessons on transitions in power within the world and the dangers that come from an emerging power attempting to subdue a dominating hegemon. The storyline of the evolving power configuration and the ensuing geopolitical rivalries form the basis of the modern-day Thucydides Trap.

Moreover, the roots of this idea go further than the ancient Greek period on its own. It should be noted that, in one form or another, similar changes of power and the conflicts that arise with it are a part of human history. The cyclical narratives that dominate the world, starting from the change in power structures, dealing with these affairs are witnessed in the rise and fall of empires and the competition between states. By analysing the history of such antecedents, one can appreciate the significance of the Thucydides Trap and lessons on modern international relations.

The origin of the Thucydides Trap can also be traced back to the attempts made by scholars to study and interpret events of history within the context of changes in power. How historians and political scientists have contributed through studying these case studies is exemplary and showcases the complexities under examination. The studies may differ, but examining the changes in superpowers and their pivotal shifts continues to present challenges to global stability. Such thorough research and attempts have always aimed at bridging the logical gaps explaining these clashes within conflict-dominating transitions of power. Through all of this, these frameworks are built to understand history and inform the present realities of international relations.

Understanding the historical context from which the Thucydides Trap arises is of paramount importance. It emerges from a rich blend of events, theories and literature, and learning about its historical construct helps us understand the intricacies of the transitions of power and its effects on international relations, cooperation and security. Furthermore, a more careful contextual approach to the Thucydides Trap enables its more contemporary versions to be understood at a deeper level, which strengthens the comprehension of forces defining the modern world order. The significance and relevance of understanding the Thucydides Trap cannot be overstated.

Key Features of Power Transition Conflicts

Power transition conflicts are one of the more common issues in international relations and involve the shift in how the relative power of the main actors in the international system is distributed. This conflict is usually associated with the rise of a challenger power to an existing hegemon, creating uncertainty and volatility within the international system. It is of greater importance to explain the main features and characteristics of power transition conflicts to understand their consequences and develop appropriate ways to mitigate them.

The essential change in shifts in the capabilities and uses of competing states gives the centre the reason for power-transition conflict. Economic, military, technological, and diplomatic relations and alliances determine the balance of international power. Asserting the rising power in itself gives recognition and acknowledgement on the world stage. At the same time, the established hegemon tries to preserve influence and further its position under the changing global reality.

Inherent tension is found between the hegemon and the emerging power in all areas, making it a distinct characteristic of power-transition conflict. It is not just in military or geopolitical terms that the animosity is expressed, but also in the economy and ideology. Interests and values of the incumbent and emerging powers clash, resulting in strategic rivalries, trade wars, conflict over land, and multiple international issues, as well as coming up with new ways of solving these issues.

In addition, the power shifts bring about conflicts with strategic ambiguities and notable chances for calibration blunders. The great power gaps and shifting power interplay greatly increase uncertainty, complicating decision-making during such transitional periods. This ambiguity, including the range of misunderstandings, misconstrued perceptions, and automatic escalation, highlights the volatility of the transition of power, relying severely on communication and management strategies for conflicts.

Additionally, conflicting dimensions in power transition conflicts bring both cooperative and competitive traits. Power transition conflicts give rise to fierce competition, predatory behaviour, and hyphen goals but also enable collaboration to achieve overlapping objectives. The conflict and cooperation blend in the change of power represents the complexity of the relations between countries with varying levels of influence, which require sophisticated diplomacy and statecraft to balance the competing demands.

In short, grasping the fundamental attributes of any power transition conflict entails studying state relations and their interdependencies alongside shifts in power and global order and stability deeply and exhaustively. By understanding the nuances accompanying such power shifts, scholars and policymakers can appreciate the challenges and opportunities accompanying these monumental shifts, as such understanding prepares them to make decisions and take actions that will implement changes in international relations.

Thucydides's Theory: Interpretations and Misinterpretations

Alison's interpretation of the Thucydides Trap accurately captures the dangers and tensions of power transitions within the international system. Yet, the broader structure of the theory does draw from Thucydides' account of the Peloponnesian War. It should also be noted that several additional layers complicate understanding this framework. There is a plethora of debates stemming from Thucydides' narrative that, at face value, seems straightforward.

To analyse Thucydides's theory, it is important to consider the entirety of his thoughts in the context of Greece's history. Thucydides's narration of the story of Athens and Sparta serves as a lesson revealing the intricacies of power, fear, and both national and international relations. Furthermore, the fact that the phrase 'Thucydides Trap' is attributed to Thucydides himself is problematic, as the phrase was first used centuries later and expands beyond the boundaries of what Thucydides set in his writings.

Inaccurate interpretations of the theory of Thucydides often stem from oversimplified approaches and cherry-picking sections of the text. One of the common mistakes that is usually made is attempting to assume what would happen in a scenario where a rising power faces an already dominant hegemon. Such critics argue that because of such interpretations, the decision-makers are stripped of their power to act and render the situation through diplomacy to diffuse the escalation of conflict. Additionally, the overly strict implementations of the Thucydides Trap can also ignore the dominant culture, economics, technology, or any other area that controls and shapes the contemporary distribution of power and, thus, the boundaries of the theory.

On the contrary, supporters of the Thucydides Trap claim that even though it is critical to consider the limitations of historical analogies, there is value in the observations made by Thucydides. As noted above, proponents cite the persistence of basic behaviours and deeper human motivations, which can be seen in power transition situations. Scholars wish to explore the detailed consequences of Thucydides and combine his understanding with modern geopolitical situations to balance his lessons against rigid conclusions.

There is a clear distinction that all interpretations of Thucydides' theory have and that neither simplistic support nor opposition to one idea is sufficient. Rather, after coming into contact with these interpretations, one will think about using historical analogies as one of the primary tools for addressing modern foreign policy problems. The following chapters of this book focus on the Thucydides Trap and its history, which is built upon a blend of contemporary structure and demands facing us today.

Implications for Modern International Relations

In the contemporary arena, the Thucydides Trap concept has dire consequences for the interactions of world powers. While the globe is in perpetual motion, the cycles of power shift conflict are an inevitability. This theory poses a paramount understanding for leaders, policymakers, and analysts trying to navigate contemporary geopolitics.

The foremost consequence of the Thucydides Trap for contemporary international relations is the increased importance of diplomacy and the need for conflict prevention. Explorations of world power politics demonstrate traps set by historical case studies and leading theoreticians. The emergence of new power in a challenge with underlying old hegemony poses great risk. Understanding this dynamic requires studying potential causes of conflicts and adequately preventing the escalation of conflict.

In addition, the idea emphasises the need to foster understanding and constructive relations between the rising and the established powers. Never yielding to unfriendly rivalries or cutthroat competition, the lessons offered by the Thucydides Trap advocate for a more constructive approach centred on cooperation, communication, and pursuing common goals. Acknowledging the inherent weaknesses and fears that both rising and declining powers continually possess allows all relevant actors to put more effort into ensuring stability in international relations.

Furthermore, as emerging economies become more important and power changes due to technological innovations, the Thucydides Trap encourages a reassessment of the established frameworks of dominance and authority in the world order. These changes require a revision of diplomatic policies alongside the endorsement of new and targeted policies that do not employ aggressive strategies to deal with the realigned balance of power.

Additionally, the consequences of the Thucydides Trap reinforce the need for multilateralism and collaborative frameworks. Due to modern economies being interwoven and global security dangers, avoiding Thucydides Trap scenarios requires alliance building, institutional aid strengthening, and fostering collective security from the onset. Such a strategy prevents unilateral moves that could increase distrust, resulting in retaliatory actions deemed destabilising.

As noted, the Thucydides Trap acts as a warning compass devoid of borders that should be responded to with strong inaction barriers. History and theory meticulously analyse power shifts and instil pragmatic ideals regarding world affairs aimed at peaceful coexistence. This heralds a cunning transition for leaders towards guided orbits that are intricately intertwined to avoid turbulent harbours.

It is important to highlight the need for leaders to welcome order, avoiding potential collisions.

Analysing Current Global Power Structures

To interpret the dynamics of the Thucydides Trap in modern times, one needs to thoroughly study how the world powers function today. The primary focus of this analysis is the constellation of alliances, rivalries, and hegemonic ambitions envisioned in 21st-century geopolitics. The world is witnessing a multipolar order with three types of actors: established powers, rising challengers, and regional powers or influencers. The interplay of these interests and influences reveals international relations as a highly sophisticated web.

When analysing world power structures, the first step is locating the principal actors of global politics. The United States, the European Union, and Russia remain traditional powers actively engaged in world politics. However, the sphere of influence is expanding with emerging powers like China, India, and Brazil. Furthermore, other powers within the Middle East and Africa are pivotal in determining the dynamics of the region while also softening the scope of global power.

Apart from military or economic might, the modern concept of power encompasses soft power, cultural influence, information technology, and diplomacy. The ability to utilise the different forms of power assists in reorganising global rankings and the fluidity of international relations.

Moreover, the global power structure change is defined by the interconnectedness of economies, the growth of global issues, and the rise of non-state actors with power. Climate change, cybersecurity, and global health are issues that can no longer be defined and solved in a state-centric way. They require collaboration and innovative approaches. Evaluating the impact of these interrelated issues on global dynamics is important to understand what could ignite conflict or cooperation in the world.

Upon further exploration of the current international relations systems, it is clear that resolving conflicts over shifting powers, as described in the Thucydides Trap, resolves more effectively when one understands the complete level of power and influence within the system. By analysing the complex networks of actors operating at the global, regional, and even local tiers, one can identify the cracks and possibilities foundational to the Thucydides Trap paradigm regarding international relations today.

Critiques and Support: Academic Discourse

The attention captured by The Thucydides Trap theory, especially in the context of international conflict and confrontation prediction, has sparked multifaceted academic discourse within and beyond its initial scope of geopolitical studies. The most important critique of this theory is the oversimplified deterministic view of a historical or geopolitical situation brimming with multidimensional factors. Critics contend that the Thucydides Trap overlooks the intricate dynamics of domestic politics, culture, and individual leaders within state relations, advocating for a comprehensive understanding of system transitions. Additionally, some scholars challenge the empirical grounding of the Thucydides Trap, noting historical instances of power transitions that occur without conflict, suggesting their peaceable nature. Such arguments illustrate the necessity to explore different historical narratives and highlight the danger posed by generalisations about conflict over power transitions. In contrast to these critiques, the defenders of Thucydides

Trap argue that no matter how unrefined the theory is regarding conflict during power transitions, it is undeniably insightful about the dangers posed by disrupting an established global order.

This camp highlights the importance placed on structural components and the socio-psychological aspects of both rising and established powers, noting those factors that have historically brought about conflict and advocating for preventive policies for risk mitigation. In addition, supporters of the Thucydides Trap theory highlight its instrumental application as a heuristic instead of a deterministic prediction, serving more to forewarn clashes than as an impetus for any arms buildup to promote adversarial relations. These disputes underscore the layers of the Thucydides Trap concept within Academia, which requires one to think critically about concepts, theories, and evidence around power transitions in today's world due to its multidisciplinary nature developed through engaging with multiple paradigms.

Significance for Policymakers and Strategists

Strategists and policymakers alike may find themselves entrapped by the evolving Thucydides Trap while navigating increasingly complex international relations. Rising and waning powers coping with the maintenance of their influence often miscalculate gaps in understanding shifts of power, which are known to create value not just for the leading nations but also for the global balance of threats and opportunities.

For decision-makers, the Thucydides Trap is a cognitive framework that encourages additional thought on strategic and diplomatic steps that need to be taken. Understanding the latent conflicts within the power transition framework enables greater anticipation of risks and allows for avoiding conflict through the proactive management of diplomacy, crisis, or war. This suggests the need for a thorough assessment of geo-strategic balances and the existence of policies shaped by the lessons of the past.

The Thucydides Trap also reinforces the importance of proactive diplomacy focused on bilateral and multilateral diplomacy to stifle conflict while increasing conflict stability. A policy decision taken too far could derail a nation's core interest, so actions should be tempered with the need for dialogue to avert the negative impact of a power shift. Proposed strategies to address the challenge of rising powers are encouraging them to foster understanding and trust with the established powers to lower tensions, thereby generating long-term peace and prosperity while promoting sustainable development.

From a strategist's perspective, the Thucydides Trap calls for reexamination and modification of military policies, alliances, and conflict resolution practices. It motivates a strategist to formulate comprehensive responses that transcend the extremes of competition or conflict when dealing with shifts in power balance. This deeply complex issue requires managing traditional and non-traditional security threats, from cybersecurity to economic dependency and border conflicts.

In addition, strategists have to consider new technology and its consequences for war, spying, and global communication networks. New developments in artificial intelligence, space, and information warfare create increased opportunities and challenges that require careful planning to maintain national security and stability during transitional power periods. These changes demand the attention of strategic planners who must carefully employ the new technology while considering the dynamics of power transition.

The primary importance of the Thucydides Trap for policymakers and strategists is its ability to combine history, contemporary relations of power, and future trajectories. This approach allows leaders to take actions aimed at avoidance, constructive engagement, and lasting security frameworks. Through understanding the Thucydides Trap, strategists and policymakers can predict the shifting global order and face it with renewed strength and commitment to global stability.

Roadmap for the Book: Themes and Questions

Before we set out on this adventure, we should set the roadmap that will take us through the stories of the Thucydides Trap and its modern-day counterparts. The book aims to address themes and questions central to the dynamics of power shifts and their impacts on the world's stability. We intend to cover different chapters, each devoted to a specific aspect of the Thucydides Trap, to give the readers the tools to understand every angle of the phenomenon. Through the themes, analyses and discussions we intend to put forth on these subjects, we hope to provide.

The first theme assessed focuses on power changes in a historical context, paying attention to pertinent history. The objectives outlined will analyse the effects of the Anglo-German Naval Arms Race or the Peloponnesian War while trying to understand the cyclical nature and dangers that power changes impose over time.

Another critical theme incorporates the new world order and China's growth as a global superpower. The objectives included will focus on China's growth, its implications for the already existing world order, the challenges that come with China's rise to superpower status, and the impact of this growth on international relations.

Competition in the international market and technological advancements are yet another example of an extreme focus. We will highlight the relationship between a country's power, trade with other countries, and technology while also showcasing how this impacts the power balance across countries.

Security threats and military aspects are equally important in our discussions. The analysis will focus on the changes in military capabilities, defence postures, and security issues that emerge from the balance of power theory and what these issues mean for the world regarding security and stability.

The analysis begins by examining conflict over international relations policy, exploring its choices and means of resolution. It then aims to define conflict mitigation strategies to aid global powers in avoiding conflict-oriented paths so that orderly peace can be possible even when the balance of power is changing.

Opportunities and challenges related to collaboration on the world stage form the second boundary of the analysis. At this point, we will focus on the potential for collaboration to address some of the most urgent global issues while considering how aggressive the relations between the world's most powerful nations are becoming.

The scenario analysis section will decant contemporary power shifts and their possible directions and outcomes to aid decision-making and provide guidance in averting impending disturbances.

Focusing on them will give rise to a variety of scenarios and forecasts, such as possible paths that may be taken owing to varying degrees of possibilities that can be set within a power shift context and the likely consequences of such shifts.

The journey ends here in the focused blend of theme-based analysis where the Thucydides Trap is defined and framed comprehensively with conclusive suggestions for scholars, policymakers, and strategists of modern times. With all themes covered, the questions raised throughout this paper will finally be answered, helping analysts make sense of the shift in structures of power and the decisions that need to be made.

3

Historical Precedents
Lessons from the Peloponnesian War

The Roots of Conflict: Athens and Sparta

The conflict between Athens and Sparta can best be understood in light of their unique political and cultural characteristics. Athens, a democracy and a major sea power, was intellectually vibrant, known for its navy, democracy, and inexhaustible creativity. It was a society that cherished freedom, public participation, and intellectual pursuits. In stark contrast, Sparta was a militaristic city-state governed by a rigid oligarchy that glorified discipline and tradition. It fiercely enforced conformity through rigorous military training and suppressed individual freedoms. These starkly different political and cultural systems fostered profound tensions which ultimately triggered the Peloponnesian War. Spartan expansion and power came into direct competition with

Athenian imperialistic tendencies. Pre-existing animosity was heightened by differing styles of governance and growing mutual distrust. It is also important to note that while Athenian democracy enabled vibrant intellectual and commercial activity fuelled by diversity of opinion, Sparta remained rigidly militarised and viewed the democratic principles of Athens as corrosive to social order.

The confrontation of these two powerful entities not only highlighted the differences in their governance structure and civic culture but also significantly impacted the lives of their citizens. The geopolitical and cultural differences deepened the root of animosity which erupted into a long-standing, devastating war. Understanding the relationship between the political frameworks and the cultures of Athens and Sparta shows that the conflict stemmed from an enduring divergence in core values and social priorities, affecting the daily lives and futures of the citizens.

Political Structures and Ideologies

The Peloponnesian War was not simply a conflict of military strength but a competition of systems and political ideas. Athens, well known for its democracy, extensive naval fleet, and rich culture, was in stark contrast to Sparta, an oligarchic society with a formidable land-based military. Every city-state's political structure deeply shaped its diplomacy, warfare, and governance. Athens, under the rule of a democratic system, had the advantage of a much more open form of government where people participated in the decision-making process, which provided them with a voice. This system created a great sense of pride and responsibility among its citizens. This system of active participation was also the case for military matters since the citizens of Athens had to defend their city, which fostered a great sense of identity and national unity.

On the other hand, the rigid elements of oligarchy and militarism characterising Sparta neglected personal freedoms in favour of strict state control, discipline, and martial training. Spartan society valued communal and austere lifestyles, moulding warriors in every sense. This unparalleled devotion to military excellence cultivated a fierce, disciplined army renowned for its resilience on the battlefield.

The enduring influence of these conflicting political ideals not only shaped the character of the Peloponnesian war, but also continues to be a compelling study within contemporary geopolitical discourse. Studying ancient political systems and their ideologies offers an enduring appreciation of the relationships between civil government, culture, and conflict. It provides a unique perspective for current and future studies in relations, warfare, politics and strategy.

Strategic Imperatives and Military Strategy

In the case of the Peloponnesian War, it becomes necessary to analyse the strategic imperatives that defined the military strategy of the war. Each Athenian and Spartan side developed certain military strategies based on their strategic imperatives and objectives. These strategic imperatives included a wide range of factors such as the geostrategic position of the state, its navy, its allies, and its supply of resources. Understanding these imperatives is crucial to comprehending the military strategies employed by each side.

Focusing on Athens, they were strong in naval power; thus, they capitalised on dominating maritime trade and projecting strategic influence throughout the Aegean Sea. Trade was needed, which led to the formation of empires. This prompted the creation of a strong navy, constructing harbours and port cities, and controlling important sea routes. Unlike Athens, Sparta was well known for its warrior culture and professional soldiers. It had strong militaristic land capabilities and steered the civilisation's focus on land warfare.

The Athenian civilisation's pursuits, such as empire expansion while conquering and subjugating city-states in the Delian League, were aligned with employing naval forces. These demonstrate a more aggressive intention. From a defensive standpoint, the Spartan civilisation's goals were to use the army to dominate the region and build strong allied power in the Peloponnesian League.

In addition, the strategic focuses also appeared in the respective Athenian and Spartan military tactics. Athenian strategies relied on sea power and employed naval blockades and amphibious assaults, projecting power and influence using Athens' unparalleled fleet. At the same time, Spartan tactics focused on infantry discipline, skilled leadership, and the building of defensive coalitions with other regional states.

The interaction of strategic imperatives and military strategy was observed more deeply in executing different campaigns and military confrontations throughout the war. These included landmark battles such as the Sphacteria and Pylos Battles, where Athenian naval power was on full display, and the land-centric Spartan Invasion of Attica, exemplifying focused military control on land operations.

Comprehending the frailties of these strategic imperatives alongside the resulting military manoeuvres deepens our understanding of the complex interactions among the geopolitical, military, and sociological forces that shaped the Peloponnesian War. Additionally, this examination sheds light on historical analysis that is profoundly useful for today's geopolitical disputes, the creation of modern context warfare, and defence policy formulation.

Key Battles and Campaigns Overview

Wars and military expeditions in ancient Greece were deeply rooted in culture and religion. The Peloponnesian War was no exception. With virtually every battle being fought strategically and tactically, the determined efforts to gain supremacy over Greece would be seen during the War of Mantinea and the ruinous battle of Plataea.

As you may already know, the War of Mantineas began in 418 BCE and displayed the tendencies of both sides to change their tactics, shifting the significance of alliances. First, the Spartans, alongside their allies, ganged up on Athens and were met with their allies—triggering an aspiring combative engagement overflowing with devastating conflict. The battle further showcased the newly developed techniques of both militaries, just as innovations and increased industrialisation took centre stage. After losing to Thebans, the Spartans were also able to claim victory at the siege of Plataea due to the intense nature of the conflict. Time and time again, warfare has shown to be easily solvable through the application of intense bombardment coupled with brutal tactics. This revealed the intricate logistical challenges of ancient armies while simultaneously stressing the importance of sieges and defensive warfare. Alongside the ruthless and politically important endeavours of fire-laden ships and devastating military precision, the siege revealed to Athens the distance and strain on democratic resources. It is without question that these led to protracted and multifaceted land and naval operational warfare.

Indeed, one way to lose supremacy over the sphere is to fully surrender to tactical shrewdness that displays raw and astonishing mayhem. The shockingly labelled 'defeated central power' would be claimed by the Athenians for themselves after they captured a breathtaking number of Spartan soldiers during the battle of Sphacteria—troubling the pre-existing balance of power.

The aforementioned battles and other campaigns

highlight the scope of strategies and the geopolitical considerations that framed the conflict of the Peloponnesian War. Each battle endured had unparalleled consequences for the participants' civilisation, which illustrates the deep intertwining of the military, political, and diplomatic factors that shaped wars in ancient times. Analysing these events strategically illustrates the timeless principles of strategy and how decisions made on the battlefield impacted military actions and diplomacy.

Diplomatic Maneuvers and Alliances

In the Peloponnesian War, diplomatic moves and alliances greatly impacted the politics and the direction of the war. In ancient Greece, the delicate balance of power among the city-states often needed resolution with respect to changing allegiances and cunning negotiations. While Athens and Sparta attempted to rally support from other cities, a new complex system of inter-state alliances formed, with every faction attempting to gain a competitive edge using their diplomacy and politics. This web of alliances was complex in that it was symbolic; however, there were significant consequences regarding resource distribution, aid in military conflicts, and control over borders.

As city-states perpetually analysed their security concerns and the advantages they might gain from aligning with one side or the other, the diplomacy system was quite complex and challenging. While some neutral city-states were subjected to intense pressure to pick a side, other optional states experienced internal conflict due to varying opinions on the most advisable action. The emerging subdivisions of these neutral states, alongside the pressure to reach a resolution, led to the sophisticated practice of diplomacy, which aided in forming and exploiting these subdivisions to form strong enough coalitions that could dominate the balance of power in favour of either Athens or Sparta.

Furthermore, the alliances formed during the Peloponnesian War not only directly impacted the battlefield; they transformed the political landscape of ancient Greece and set the stage for future wars. Some alliances were forged based on shared interests and collective ideologies, while others were formed out of practical rationales and contingency plans. All treaties made during the wars and negotiations reveal the complicated nature of diplomacy in ancient times and highlight the importance of diplomatic strategy even in modern politics and international relations.

In addition, the study of these alliances sheds light on the advantages and disadvantages associated with coalition-building endeavours. Even in the ancient world, city-states had to deal with problems of trust, betrayal, and fragile power balances. Insights gained from the diplomatic activities from this period can both warn and motivate policymakers and diplomats today. Analysing the strategies employed to create and maintain alliances during the Peloponnesian War gives insight into how diplomacy influences the results of sustained conflicts and the geopolitical arena.

Economic Factors and Resource Management

The Peloponnesian War was both a military clash and a conflict of economic interests and resource management. Both cities sought to capitalise on their economic clout and access to resources to gain the upper hand during the war. Considering how the Athenian Empire was founded on maritime trade and tribute from most of their subject allies, it is no wonder that this incredible economic powerhouse provided Athens with sufficient funds. This enabled Athens to finance a formidable navy, maintain a large professional army, and fund ambitious building projects such as the famous Acropolis. On the other hand, Sparta primarily relied on the labour of the working-class helots and the support of its allies in the Peloponnesian League. While Sparta's economy was geared towards supporting its renowned military prowess, it did not possess the financial resources and infrastructure available in Athens.

The war also affected Ancient Greece's economy in numerous ways. It blocked city-state trade and further worsened intra-Athenian relationships. Both sides of the war suffered from poor resource allocation during prolonged fighting. The strained effort for resource allocation during the protracted attempts at warfare signifies how closely integrated economic power, war-making capabilities, and the ability to endure struggle were.

Wars can be attributed to Economics and Politics

equally, mandating correct resource allocation as a prerequisite symbolic for success. Gaining essential resources, particularly food, timber for shipbuilding, and financial aid, weaponised both Athens and Sparta, which helped both sides strategically and initially shackled them. Additionally, the case of the failed expedition to Syracuse illustrated the fundamental importance of careful resource allocation by emphasising the wartime distortion of societal needs.

Aside from the direct consequences to the economy, the Peloponnesian War inflicted lasting changes on the economic policies and frameworks of Ancient Greece. The conflict required new systems of economic administration, including the management of taxation and public finances, which later contributed to the evolution of economic control. As such, the conflict fought during the Peloponnesian War over economic control and resource management provides a profound understanding of the relationship between economy, war, and social strength.

Leadership and Decision-Making Dynamics

During the prolonged conflict known as the Peloponnesian War, the powerful city-states of Athens and Sparta fought for supremacy, each with varying systems of both ruling and governance. The leadership dynamics and decision-making processes heavily influenced strategy and the outcomes of the war. Cleon and Pericles, for instance, were able to shift the whole Athenian empire into a form of democracy, which completely transformed how the Athenian side of the war was conducted due to the impacts of Pericles and Cleon creating an empire. The Athenian System, as well as other democratic empires, can achieve so much as they use public debates and discussions, which helps in coming up with solutions and assists in creating quite an aggressive war cabinet. Multiple energetic citizens can help the war cabinet diplomatically overcome their foes. Sparta, on the other hand, had an oligarchic system as they functioned under two shoguns and a senile council, tending to be slow, conservative, and even, at times, remorseless in their ways of thinking. With a blend of contrasting governing styles, both city-states emerged with incompatible styles of resource allocation, military planning, alliance forming, and execution. To appreciate modern geopolitical conflicts, analysing and studying their leadership approaches spanning military, strategic, and diplomatic relations is imperative.

The role of leadership and individual character traits highly influenced the outcome of the Peloponnesian War. The strategic and persuasive skills of Athenian leaders like Alcibiades and Nicias greatly affected the outcome of military plans and diplomatic negotiations. They illustrate the relationships between warfare and governance. Sparta's leaders like Brasidas and Lysander had a more traditionalist and martial leadership approach that guided their distinct decision-making styles. These historical personalities are remarkable examples of how individual leadership characteristics affect the conduct and results of wars.

Analysing decision-making processes at coalition and alliance levels reveals the myriad connections that determined the development of the war. Joint military operations and diplomatic activities had dependencies due to communication and trust, which required active coordination. The ability to manage inter-state rivalries significantly impacted the momentum of the conflict.

An important understanding is obtained from exploring the gaps and weaknesses of the decision-making of both sides. Strategic blunders, diplomacy failures, and internal strife highlight the need for sound leadership and cohesive decision-making during protracted conflicts. In addition, the analysis of unexpected and external pressures needs to be conducted to understand how these challenges tested the leaders and to grasp the lessons regarding statecraft's endurance and frailty.

Studying the Peloponnesian War and its leaders reveals the complex intertwining of politics, military strategy, and human behaviour, decisively shaping international relations. It becomes evident that ancient leaders left insightful and detrimental blueprints on their civilisations through their decision-making frameworks, and assessing their reigns offers vital insights for modern civilisation camouflaged in the shifting paradigms of global power.

Impact on Greek Civilisation and Beyond

The effects of the Peloponnesian War are noted not

only from the battlefield perspective but are also widely recognised throughout Greek civilisation and history for hundreds of years thereafter. Mostly, the clash between Athens and Sparta changed the dynamics of ancient Greece on a political level, marking the change of Athenian rule into Spartan rule. The city-states had to deal with wars for prolonged periods, which consumed their resources completely. This and the resentment and disillusionment bound to follow amongst the citizens made matters even worse. While the city-states were bound to fall, external forces also looked towards exploiting them. The collapse of the system that balanced the power brought forth conflict and strife. This era was later known for the rise of Macedon under Philip II and, after him, Alexander the Great. Other than the Peloponnesian War, these were some of the dominant reasons the democracy withdrew its further supporting hand and shield, consequently showing the weaknesses of democratic rule. This phenomenon became known as 'statehood and political science' in historical textbooks.

Furthermore, the overwhelming destruction that the war caused, regarding the loss of life, led to a reevaluation of preexisting moral frameworks. This resulted in cynicism that permeated the intellectual sentiment of the era. This sentiment would give rise to self-reflection that transformed philosophical study and reasoning for centuries after. The implications of the Peloponnesian War were felt beyond Greece and changed power relations worldwide. This conflict fundamentally shifted the political landscape as the newly empowered city-states and emerging kingdoms from the Greek Hellenistic age had to grapple with complex relations of both alliances and rivalries for optimal power in the region. The Hellenistic civilisation that ensued created a fusion of cultures through military expansion, greatly enhancing art, literature, and philosophy. Such advances would profoundly shape the foundation of Western civilisation. These globally transformative effects of the war and insights into its impact on Greek civilisation justify the Peloponnesian War as one of the most important conflicts in history.

Historiographical Perspectives

There is a wide range of diverse interpretations regarding the historiography of the Peloponnesian War between ancient and modern historians. The earliest work was written by Thucydides, who is considered the first person to write about history narratively. It describes this era of conflict, detailing sociopolitical sympathies, struggles for power, conflicts and their repercussions on civilisation, and the psychology of people. States and individuals have rational incentives, which are crucial in analyses, and have fostered the growth of realism in international relations, a doctrine that many other theorists have influenced. Moreover, the foundational work that enriches our understanding of the longstanding conflict is by Herodotus, who discusses the geopolitical state before the war. Medieval Town and Country complemented him with its moralistic interpretation of the war's necessity, where rulers wanted to extract political meaning for moral objectives from the conflict to teach contemporary governance and statecraft. In our contemporary era of modernity, the conflict of the war is most intensely discussed for having socio-economic reasons that, according to a Marxist point of view, disregard progress with cultural developments and consider ideological advancement as mere struggle. The existence of revisionists has altered the established view on other important events, which have been termed mistakes, along with the individuals who were meant to guide people through them.

Furthermore, postcolonial and feminist theories have focused on non-elite individuals on the periphery of social hierarchies and how gender constructs affect their experiences during war, highlighting overlooked narratives. The changing nature of historiographical methods has created a rich tapestry of interpretations and invited further research and critique. Despite the continual discovery of new evidence and the application of novel approaches, the historiography of the Peloponnesian War remains an active and shifting field, revealing the complex interconnections of ancient history with current global issues and interstate relations.

Lessons for Modern Geopolitical Strategies

Analysing the Peloponnesian War can be particularly insightful for contemporary international relations and global geopolitics. Understanding this ancient conflict is essential as it reveals important aspects of political power, rivalry, diplomacy, and strategy, which are vital today for nations' emerging policies and actions towards one another.

Understanding the Peloponnesian War prompts one to ponder how national militaries, economies, and politics intersect. The collision of these factors is no less complicated than contemporary global competition, so considering all angles is essential, especially in the ever-growing suzerain-vassal rivalry.

The paradox of alliances and coalitions provides insights into their potential merits and vulnerabilities. Modern policymakers and strategists can learn to balance conflicts of interest regarding coalition complications and discrepancy management throughout shifting world power dynamics.

Policymakers are reminded why ideology and culture still bear weight in relations between states and moderates, such as the enforcement of democracy in geopolitics and soft power-motivated ancient Greek actors. The ancient war taught us not only to focus on the forces trying to manipulate and control us but to blend the different with constituents used to operate covertly and appeal to our chosen objectives.

Moreover, the Peloponnesian War stands out as a powerful proxy for the consequences of unilateral military action, as it demonstrates how the snare of unilateralism and overreliance on military dominance often leads to multifaceted, extended conflicts. Contemporary policymakers studying the repercussions of unchecked aggressive force and hegemonic aspirations are educated on the consequences of recklessness and the importance of sensible strategic thinking well ahead into the future.

In conclusion, studying the Peloponnesian War will undoubtedly prove insightful as it serves to teach valuable lessons about history, strategy, and modern-day geopolitics. Through rigorous examination of the intricacies of this ancient conflict, modern-day strategists appreciate the complexities of power and diplomacy and the value of careful planning and prudent decision-making for fostering healthy international relations.

4

Rivalry and Cooperation
The Anglo-German Naval Arms Race

Introduction to the Naval Arms Race

The naval arms clash between Britain and Germany at the beginning of the 20th century was not just a conflict, but a strategic manifestation of their geopolitical stresses and strategies. Both countries vigorously pursued naval power, recognising it as a fundamental factor for trade and global influence, and even a prerequisite for becoming a world superpower. This dispute can be explained as a complex mixture of factors like intense nationalism, imperialist expansion, multifaceted competition for resources, and changing power dynamics in Europe. With the Industrial Revolution came technological advancements, resulting in both nations competing to claim supremacy over the seas, leading to problematic and militaristic enhancements of naval fleets. Now combine these factors with fierce rivalries due to economic disputes, colonial powers, and alliances among European countries. These factors together created a volatile situation that gave rise to the intensification of the naval arms race. Notably, the naval arms race was not simply an attempt at the projection of might; it was equally a projection of grand strategy and politics. The great emphasis on naval expansion showed what each country wanted in world politics: control over trade routes and dominion over essential overseas minerals, trade colonies, and resources and markets.

Additionally, the arms race of naval fleets highlighted the more fragile aspects of international relations, including the possibility of militarised escalation. This serves as a reminder of the vulnerabilities existing within the geopolitical framework. Incorporating the naval arms race into international competition undoubtedly exposed and heightened the interwoven rivalries in world politics in the pre-World War I period. The race encapsulated the complex militaristic tensions and fervent nationalism that had seized the world, eventually altering the trajectory of global history.

The Genesis of Anglo-German Tensions

The period of growing hostility between Great Britain and Germany had been a culmination of multiple historical events. We can pinpoint the origin of Anglo-German tensions to the aggressive rise of German industrial and military power, which came in the late nineteenth and early twentieth century and was put on a collision course against British naval supremacy. As a result, Germany became embroiled in a struggle for global dominance, prompting a long-lasting conflict for maritime power, thereby leading to a rapid shift in the global balance of power.

Underlying this growing antagonism were complex historical grievances and competing national ambitions. Britain's naval dominance was directly challenged by Germany's rapid industrialisation and economic expansion during the reign of Kaiser Wilhelm II. Germany's powerful naval construction alongside Admiral Alfred von Tirpitz's ambitious shipbuilding programmes fuelled apprehensions within British strategic circles. There was the ever-present suspicion that a resurgent Germany could cripple British maritime interests and colonial possessions, which escalated the already existing atmosphere of suspicion and caution in London.

The intricate web of alliances and geopolitical tensions further fueled the growing Anglo-German rivalry. The Entente of France and Russia, later joined by Britain, acted as a counterbalance to the Triple Alliance of Germany, Austria-Hungary, and Italy. This shift in alliances heightened existing tension, fracturing Europe's already delicate balance of power. The destabilising impact of Anglo-German naval competition raised the stakes, underscoring the underlying tension created by the expanding web of alliances in the region.

Also important were the cultural and ideological factors that shaped Anglo-German relations during this period. Nationalist fervour and imperial desires, blended with fears of encirclement or potential isolation, influenced the conversations on naval policies and maritime defence. New narratives emerged depicting each nation as a protector of freedom and civilisation pitted against the other's aspiring ambitions. This created an environment of deep suspicion, increasing the chances of an arms race out of perceived vulnerability and self-preservation.

Increased resentment and simmering tensions prepared the battleground, giving rise to an intense phase of naval rivalry, power politics, and relentless competition, which would alter the course of the two nations and the world's geopolitical dynamic.

Economic and Industrial Capacity

The naval rivalry between Great Britain and Germany was not merely a display of militaristic competitiveness, but a reflection of their economic and industrial prowess. Both nations understood that expanding their naval armaments was a direct consequence of their economic output and the value of their industries. The war of attrition on the naval fleet necessitated, or at the very least encouraged, the expenditure of resources and investment in sophisticated infrastructure.

Britain, balancing its colonial possessions with a developed industry, emerged as a formidable global power. Its trade capabilities alongside the industry level allowed for the establishment of an industrial base, enabling Britain to support its naval military. Compared to other nations, Britain possessed an advantage over its competitors due to its distinct industrial capabilities and economy, which was further enhanced by available raw materials in the colonies and an upper-tier shipbuilding industry, bolstering its naval supremacy.

Simultaneously, Germany, an emerging industrial powerhouse, sought to leverage its growing economic strength to construct advanced naval vessels to contend with British naval dominance. The country's expansion in the manufacturing and steel industries allowed Germany to invest in warships, and enhanced commercial trade further necessitated the need for naval defence to protect vital resources.

Both countries aided in fuelling the naval arms race, which required investments in modernising shipyards, expanding industry, and improving infrastructure. Aside from naval prowess, steel, engine manufacturing, and logistical support were enhanced as a by-product of construction industry development. With the increased competition, both countries focused on R&D in design, propulsion, and armament technology as an indicator of superiority over one another, signifying the differences in economic and naval power between nations.

The economic and industrial factors of the naval arms race profoundly impacted national economies, employment, and societal frameworks. The shipbuilding and peripheral industries experienced a remarkable upsurge in demand for specialised labour, which increased economic activity and employment in certain regions. Governments adopted strategies aimed at subsidising and promoting innovation within their shipbuilding industries.

Thus, Britain and Germany fueled the Anglo-German naval arms race primarily because of both nations' industrial and economic capabilities. Their growing infrastructure, advanced technology, skilled labour, and almost everything else that British and German business could offer signalled that there was a relationship between naval armament and fuel for the economy. This evolving relationship dramatically influenced several global and economic policies during this phase of history.

Technological Advancements in Naval Warfare

Before the Anglo-German naval arms race, the advancements in naval warfare technology were crucial in changing the face of competition among maritime nations. The shifts in technology played a major part in the strategies and capabilities of the naval powers during that time. One of the biggest advancements was the shift from coal-powered ships to oil-powered vessels because it greatly enhanced both speed and range while decreasing logistical constraints. There was increased flexibility for naval operations because greater distances could be covered in less time, expanding their influence across the seas.

Moreover, the development of long-range naval artillery and torpedo systems resulted in more potent armaments, which changed the dynamics of naval warfare. The enhanced precision and range of naval weaponry posed numerous challenges and prospects for naval strategists, altering their preconceived perspectives on tactics and doctrines. Moreover, armour and hull design advancements also improved the vessels' durability, allowing naval fleets to survive highly hostile environments.

The development of wireless communication technology transformed naval operations by allowing for the exchange of information and coordination even over long distances. This improved the efficiency of naval fleet command and control, increasing their responsiveness and flexibility during engagements. The important role of technological progress in naval warfare highlighted the impact of the relationship between industry, science, and military strategy, which encouraged innovation and competition among maritime powers.

Also, aviation application in naval warfare is an enhancement that increases naval forces' scope and extent. Introducing aircraft carriers and flying boats increased the strategic scope of sea battles by providing additional means for reconnaissance, striking, and guarding the fleet. The synergy of aviation with naval forces changed the maritime battleground and created the need for fundamental changes in naval strategies and operational tactics.

To summarise, the period before the Anglo-German naval arms race was distinguished by marked changes in naval technology that changed the zenith of maritime power projection. Such advancements increased the lethality and effectiveness of naval forces but also caused strategic shifts and changes in naval warfare doctrine, bringing the entire world towards an era of increased competitiveness and tension at sea.

Diplomatic Maneuvers and Agreements

The Anglo-German naval race was not only a competition of military prowess and technical achievement but also an intricate struggle of diplomacy for relative power and safety. Arms races were created due to rivalry and competition. Diplomacy's contribution in this regard is critical since both sides tried to manoeuvre in advance through the network of alliances, treaties, and agreements to optimise their positions without defaulting to open conflict. Central to this diplomatic tussle were expedient agreements and strategic discourse, often setting the pace of naval arms construction.

Important diplomatic measures included the creation of several naval treaties, such as the Anglo-German naval agreement of 1900, which was intended to reduce the strain caused by the competition by restraining naval arms races. As it frequently happened, however, while both states attempted to sidestep each other and take greater advantage of the agreements, new competitions inched both nations towards even more rivalry. In parallel, other states were also approached within diplomacy so that Britain and Germany could enhance or consolidate their circles of alliance and influence.

These diplomatic efforts affected the immediate naval competition and the greater geopolitical order of Europe and beyond. Shifts in the balance of power were caused by diplomatic defeats and victories, which affected not only the arms race but also international relations. The relationship between diplomacy, militarisation, and public opinion contributed to this volatile environment, as every action taken by one side was met with a counteraction from the other side, constantly heightening tensions.

Also, these diplomatic actions, in addition to being bilateral, impacted wider alliances and broader power relations. The intertwining diplomacy of the various belligerents and their manoeuvrings during the naval arms race suggest that diplomacy prepared the stage for alliances and coalitions that would culminate in a fierce world war.

Key Figures and Their Influence

During the Anglo-German naval arms race, various individuals from either side wielded influence to formulate policies in Britain and Germany. Britain had Admiral John Fisher, the First Sea Lord of the Royal Navy, who became an aggressive expansionist and modernistic supporter of the navy. English naval strategy and resource allocation in the arms race were greatly impacted by Fisher's advocacy for new classes of battleships and greater naval resources. Other influential figures include Fisher's successor as the First Lord of the Admiralty, Winston Churchill, who later served as Prime Minister. He also countered German naval expansion by strengthening resources, British naval power, and military expenditure. On the German side, Admiral Alfred von Tirpitz, the State Secretary of the Imperial Naval Office, aggressively supported German armament policy, greatly expanding expectations for fleet construction and developing advanced naval doctrine. Germany's naval policies were significantly influenced by von Tirpitz's vision and determination, which greatly increased Britain's focus on Germany.

In addition, political figures such as Kaiser Wilhelm II or King Edward VII of Britain had significant power as their diplomatic actions and public utterances affected the naval arms competition and influenced how the nations perceived their military power and national prestige. The combination of these chief actors and their respective strategic outlooks, as well as the context of the relevant international setting, underscored the intricate aspects of the Anglo-German naval arms race, which also served as a paradigm for the complexities of the international system, the relationship between states, and competition for maritime strength. Examining the roles and influence of these key actors shows that their consequences were not only felt within their span of existence but profoundly altered policies related to naval warfare strategy, international politics, and the continental history of the twentieth century.

Effects on Domestic Policies

The maritime arms race between Britain and Germany had serious implications for the domestic policies of both countries. The competition adjusted both the industrial policies and the budget plans. Militaristic spending grew consistently from both sides. This sparked vigorous disputes in Parliament for Britain, causing further investment in defence and prioritisation of national security. The Parliament's petitions for spending and construction of new naval ships also put additional pressure on the German government. These results forced changes in many parts of the economy, including employment, infrastructure, and technological innovation.

Furthermore, the international competition shaped the social and cultural aspects of the countries involved. Patriotism became rampant as everyone supported their country's expansion of naval forces. Citizens were constantly bombarded by propaganda, which further galvanised them to support their side. The opposition's potential threat unified the people, enforcing discipline and instilling focus towards the issue at hand.

Equally, the effects on domestic politics were significant. The naval arms race became a pivotal issue during elections, shaping campaign strategies, influencing voter sentiments, and impacting political party platforms. Political leaders used the international tensions to gain public support and demonstrate their willingness to protect the state's interests. Relations and alliances were systematically brokered to secure diplomatic support and strategic gain, thus deepening the domestic implications of the hegemonic struggle.

Moreover, the STEM workforce had to be trained in developing and adopting new technologies to address arms race-driven requirements. The public-private partnership with the military complex focused on innovation in naval engineering, weapons, and maritime strategy, which required heightened attention to STEM subjects and specialised skills. The arms race changed the educational and vocational training paradigms, making them more responsive to industry, thus enhancing the perception of science and technology in education.

To conclude, the Anglo-German naval arms race impacted a wide spectrum of domestic policies, redefining the primary focus of the economy, the attitude of society, and government responses. The deep consequences of the rival contest brought to light a new side of the interplay between military rivalry and the internal workings of nations, profoundly shaping the course of history.

Public Perception and Nationalism

The public perception and the nationalist sentiments significantly influenced how the Anglo-German Naval Arms Race was handled. This case study serves as a profound example of how two countries engaged in propaganda and twisted the perception of the other country to pose a threat to both economic prosperity and security. In Britain, through speeches and publications, the media stirred up nationalistic feelings that Britain had to maintain its maritime prowess and safeguard British interests. As Britain was presented as an aggressive and expansionist power, patriotic emotions surged, and the public felt it was their nationalistic duty to defend the Empire.

Likewise, the German media and government had to employ nationalistic discourse to garner public support for the naval arms build-up. This story lacked focus on why German interests had to be defended and why Germany needed to emerge as a significant player in the global arena. The narrative used nationalism to mobilise people under a single slogan, which claimed that Germany was under siege and that naval expansion had to be defended.

The growth of nationalism also affected society by changing the public narrative and perception of the arms race. It made the tensions between the two countries more pronounced, causing the growth of anti-foreign sentiment alongside patriotic zeal. The nationalist trends made it difficult to argue rationally or solve issues diplomatically, making compromises even harder.

Moreover, the world was affected by the rationale behind nationalism and the public's perception domestically, as it reshaped countries' politics and alliances. National narratives pivoting around power and dominance hardened trust issues, bypassing any conciliatory approaches. Intensifying rhetoric and intense nationalism made it increasingly unlikely to settle the escalated tensions peacefully, worsening the pre-existing geopolitical friction that contributed to World War One.

Revisiting the lessons of this period in history, one observes that the relationship between public opinion and nationalism is a case study of the extent to which collective perceptions and sentiments can influence international relations. For strategies to respond to current problems and potential conflicts, it is important to appreciate how nationalism has shaped strategic competition. Assessing the interplay between public opinion and nationalism during the Anglo-German naval arms race reveals more about the relations between domestic sentiments and international power relations.

Outcomes and Consequences

The Anglo-German naval arms race produced and resulted in massive outcomes, including, but not limited to, an impact throughout Europe and far beyond. This strife was marked by significantly escalating geopolitical and military competition caused by the underlying complex power struggles with rising nationalist sentiments. Not only did enduring competition for naval dominance between the two countries strain international relations, but the accompanying wave of continental militarisation and strained relations also resulted in increased tension throughout the continent.

The most striking outcomes of the naval arms race include the engrained hatred and mistrust between Britain and Germany. This atmosphere of distrust circulated through all political interactions and the formulation of policies, fuelling an insecurity rivalry. The degree of militarisation and the investments in naval capabilities also highlighted the instability of international relations during this time.

With the continuous jitters that came with the naval arms race, a heavy strain was put on both countries' economic and industrial capabilities. The expenditure of funds in naval expansion needed to come from somewhere, and social welfare programmes, eventually leading to infrastructure development, became the unfortunate target. In addition to all that, the relentless pursuit of naval dominance put a lot of strain on the domestic socio-economic sphere, nurturing a hyper-nationalistic mindset while draining resources that could have been set aside to address the fundamental challenges of society instead.

Alongside the internal factors intertwined, the unprovoked pursuit of naval capabilities drastically transformed Europe's geopolitical identity. The shifting balance created an underlying tension which made it difficult to negotiate diplomatically, thus reshaping the entire dimension of international relations. The numerous alliances and ententes showcased the intricate network of interests, fears, and expectations that influenced every nation to make a decisive call.

In addition, the results of the Anglo-German naval arms race had lasting historical outcomes which serve as lessons for today's strategic studies. The consequences of exacerbated militarisation and the struggle for supremacy of the seas have highlighted the potential volatility within contention for power on the international stage.

The consequences of the Anglo-German naval arms race are still relevant today. They reflect on the geopolitical rivalry of the past and the importance of naval forces in contemporary policies. The unfiltered consequences of such conflicts inform modern strategic policy assessments, demonstrating that today's struggles cannot be divorced from history.

Lessons Learned and Contemporary Relevance

The Anglo-German naval arms race of the early 20th century illustrates issues that still greatly affect contemporary geopolitical conversations. One lesson learned from this episode of history is the lack of control over competitive relations between two parties and its consequences, which often leads to disaster. The unchecked escalation of military capabilities, coupled with nationalist fervour and escalating tension, miscalculation, and the ultimate world conflict - WW1, leads us to understand that diplomacy, cooperation, and effective rivalry management are key in preventing armed struggle. Also, naval power as the foremost military component of a nation's security policy proves the arms race of the early century still holds relevance today, as might is a continued necessity for powerful states vying for global influence. In comparing modern-day conflicts over territory, naval superiority, and state sovereignty, the Anglo-German naval arms race example proves useful as one attempt to grasp the harsh reality of imperialistic political manoeuvres and military posturing. Not to mention, there is a dire need for stability, order, and a well-defined hierarchy, and through leveraging such pointers, strategists emerge successful. The relevance of such arms rivalries to contemporary geopolitics, especially when considering contested waters and naval power competitions, suggests politicians should exercise strategic forethought.

Apart from the lessons learned, the Anglo-German naval arms race provides a crucial study of the competition of arms in the context of its resources and the economy. The notable strain on the steam economy, aggravated by the construction of naval industries, was a major factor in creating resentment and suspicion towards competitive powers. This exemplifies the socio-economic consequences that arise in the struggle for military power during competition and the exact need for resource concentration toward the national security aims of a state. Furthermore, the persisting impacts of the arms race between Britain and Germany underscore the necessity to resolve disputes to develop constructive relationships without prior associations. These rivals, once understood, accepted, and embraced through bold diplomacy, confidence-building exercises, and cooperative policy development, aided in easing those relations. At a time of heightened competition and shifting centres of power, the world is experiencing the enduring lessons of the Anglo-German naval arms race.

5

Transitions of Power
The US-UK Example Post-WWII

The End of the British Empire: Decline and Transformation

The might of the British Empire began to lose its grip on the feared colonial power after the Second World War. The extensive expenditures inflicted by the global conflict on Britain, in combination with the war decolonisation, triggered a new era in global governance. It served as the beginning of the dismantling of the dominant British imperialism after the middle colonial infrastructure was swiftly broken down with the various independence struggles in Asia, Africa, and the Middle East.

Britain was confronting many domestic problems, such as economic depletion and post-war inflation. Additionally, the British economy had to deal with a crippling wartime debt that was further compounded by the colonised regions' growing nationalism. The ever-increasing demand for self-ruled governance posed challenges and shifted the dynamics in the British imperial government.

The dramatic geopolitical impacts that British colonies sought to claim on the world stage after decolonisation were arguably one of Britain's greatest problems in foreign policy and diplomacy. Losing essential military bases and resources fundamentally changed the world power Britain once was. This not only redirected British foreign relations but fundamentally changed the strategy Britain took regarding global conflict.

Britain was left in shambles, with the United States rising as the world's dominant power. The British Empire had to accept the reality that American influence was changing the world at a rapid pace. The new region welcomed US authority in world affairs through the Marshall Plan and the formation of international institutions. The decline of the British Empire emphasised the never-ending attempts at managing post-colonial transitions but also resulted in shifting grounds for new strategies of international relations and diplomacy.

US Global Ascendancy: From Isolation to Dominance

The US global ascendancy marks a period post World War II where the USA claimed its global dominance after transforming from an isolated economy. The United States was driven to take centre stage through the remodellings in international politics, economics, and security through a combination of shifts in forces, including economic growth, technological advancements, and the geopolitical landscape. During this crucial period, the United States was situated at a removed geographic distance, had limited engagement in global matters, and was referred to as a principal instructor of the hegemonic capitulation post-war alignment.

The war saw major reconstruction operations, leading to the USA becoming the world's global leader as the sole driving power of the Marshall Plan. The world's sole superpower led in rebuilding devastated countries, showcasing its almighty economic and humanitarian viewpoint while force-branding its control on Earth. The creation of centres like The United Nations and Bretton Woods system reflected the USA's emergency intent and resolve to bring unity and order.

In addition, the United States experienced rapid acceleration in industries and technological changes, further consolidating its supremacy. The industrial innovations of the US, which included the development of nuclear energy, aerospace technology, and the growth of multinational corporations, ensured that it not only amplified its hard power but also revealed its unparalleled ability to modernise and control the world. American innovation's imprint was broad in many other fields, including science, technology, entertainment, and consumerism, which significantly boosted the image of the US as a dominating global trendsetter.

At the same time, the US also took diplomatic steps for collective security that led to the creation of important alliances like NATO. These alliances acted as supporting structures of order, demonstrating the US's dedication to maintaining the international system and countering any possible challengers. On the other hand, the US also faced other difficult geopolitical problems, such as the standoff in the Cold War, where it emerged as the champion of democracy and the ideological fight against communism.

During the post-war period, the United States's ascent as a superpower was anchored by its economy and industry. The dominance of the US dollar as a global reserve currency and free trade enabled America's economic supremacy to facilitate a transformational shift in trade worldwide. The US bolstered American multinational corporations, which exacerbated the spread of American influence and transformed international supply and capital markets.

In the sphere of defence, the United States sought to foster international order and world peace while building military strength to defend its title as a global superpower. This change, which relied heavily on spending in military and defence technology, led America to assume the role of global security provider, tasked with the offence of anti-access, a term that refers to the prevention of an adversary's use of a particular area, freedom of maritime traffic, and alliance consolidation among the allied nations.

Rising US supremacy marks a new chapter in international relations as it embodies America's sheer power and the impact of its active role in global affairs. The post-war era saw the US take centre stage, which dramatically changed relations between countries and shifted the roles of world order governance, security, and economics.

The Special Relationship: Evolution and Significance

The special relationship between the United States and the United Kingdom has been an active element in international diplomacy since World War II and can be regarded as a key alliance formed from shared values and close collaboration during the war. Its evolution can be traced through various geopolitical shifts that forged a bond that transcended strategic interests. The special relationship embodies a remarkable blend of political, economic, and cultural ties that have shaped global affairs for decades. It is marked by sharing intelligence, defence cooperation, and several other partnerships with far-reaching implications.

The special relationship has more significance than is often recognised. It tremendously influenced policy decisions across the Atlantic and served as a trailblazer for multilateral engagement. Its wider impact is evident in joint military endeavours, coordinated diplomacy, and collaboration on pressing international challenges. In addition, the partnership extends beyond government to embrace societal, academic, and people-to-people links, which foster goodwill and mutual understanding.

July 23, 1948, marks the date of the special relationship. Starting with joint efforts in Thames Estuary aircraft carrier construction, it saw growing cooperation throughout the British post-war defence reductions and allied naval arms races. While adjusting to new scenarios in the Cold War, the collapse of the Soviet Union, and the shift in the focus of security threats.

The sustenance of this alliance has withstood the test of time, strengthening the shared values of democracy, human rights, and a free economy. The relationship between the US and the UK has withstood the test of time regarding conflict and peace and has developed into a template for how countries can positively engage with each other.

Moreover, considering the context of current relations in the world, special focus is needed on the special relationship and its expected future development. The USA and UK deal with new problems such as cybersecurity and climate change, and the alliance proves its reliability. In addition, the special relationship is a driving force for uniting Europe and America and enables more efficient action in the globalised world. In other words, the US-UK special relationship, in its advancement and importance, portrays the enduring value of strategic partnerships in the international arena.

Economic Realignment: The Bretton Woods System

The Allied powers came together after the WWII economy almost collapsed. To facilitate this new international order, they held the 1944 Bretton Woods Conference. During the conference, representatives of the 44 Allied nations constructed a framework that would serve as monetary and financial relations post-war. As a result of this, the Bretton Woods System was established, which caused a fundamental change from what existed before the war.

One of the most important changes in the Bretton Woods System was the establishment of the International Monetary Fund (IMF) and the World Bank. Both institutions were intended to strengthen cooperation between international economies and fill the financial gaps necessary to rebuild economies devastated during the war. The banks would also support equal opportunities for all member nations. Creating a country that implemented a dollar exchange currency system allowed the United States to utilise gold exchange. Due to its role, the US aimed to advance investment towards the international market.

The Bretton Woods System also indicates increasing US dominance as a world economy. The United States was one of the foremost adopters and advocates of the system, allocating a significant amount of financial aid toward it and ensuring its influence on its design. The

World Bank and International Monetary Fund were established to formally acknowledge US leadership, which was incorporated into them. With the US industrial might fully functional after the war, its dollar was established in the Bretton Woods System as a central reserve currency. This led to simultaneous advancements for America and Wisconsin Sawmills, which competed for supremacy in the global lumber market and the backbone of the US economy.

As early as the 1960s, however, problems began with underwriting quotas allocated to the US, with bloc adjustments occurring in the mid-1960s. These caused growing imbalances along with the increased spending of the US dollar on international relations and military expenditures. This resulted in greater speculation against the American currency. Consequently, these wealthy nations colluded to form policies to control the Americans, which by the mid-1970s triggered new policies to weaken the American-controlled Fixed Exchange Rate System set up at Bretton Woods. By the mid-70s, it had been fully transformed into a Fixed Rate System with free-floating exchange rates, and following a period of stagnation, led to uncontrolled exchange rates.

Regardless, the legacy of the Bretton Woods System persists today as it created a framework for other forms of international cooperation regarding issues such as monetary policy and development finance. Its basic tenets remain relevant to debates about global economic governance and the control of international financial relations, marking it as a trend-setting event in shaping history and economic order.

Military Alliances and NATO's Role

The Second World War led to a profound transformation in the geopolitical framework. During this period, military alliances became the foundational element of international security. This was epitomised by the formation of the North Atlantic Treaty Organization (NATO) in 1949, which aimed at protecting the coalition's collective defence and deterrence posture against encroaching threats.

While analysing NATO's impact on contemporary international relations, one must not overlook the significance of the organisation. NATO was created in response to what was considered to be the Soviet Union's threat and its expansionist policies into Europe. NATO was designed to counter the Soviet Union by bringing together nations willing to defend each other against attacks that might occur and to combat the spread of communism to other nations while upholding democracy.

The idea of NATO's collective defence helped shape the organisation's effectiveness. One of its core principles was that an attack on one member would invoke an attack on all. This fundamental idea acted as a bulwark against aggression and simultaneously improved trust and collaboration within NATO member states, creating increased durability.

Moreover, NATO was essential in developing standardised military capabilities and interoperability among the members. NATO's joint exercises, intelligence sharing, and development of defence policies facilitated integration by establishing national armed forces, improving the potential for unified action in response to dangers.

The organisation also helped resolve disputes and maintain diplomacy, acting as a platform where member states would participate in dialogue and collaborate, increasing peace and reducing tension within Europe and beyond.

NATO provided a crucial military defence against Soviet expansionism and served as a buffer for countries fearing the spread of communism. The organisation's strongest aspect was its unified defence, which preserved stability, reduced conflict escalation, and provided predictability in a volatile international situation.

To sum up, NATO has influenced the military alliances formed today and preserved peace and security in the post-WWI2 era. NATO advanced unity and cooperation and even deterred conflict that was budding between member states while simultaneously serving international order and stability.

Cultural Change: The Spread of Americanism

The rise of American culture (both socially and economically) began forcefully appearing on the global pedestal after the Second World War and is often recognised as the term 'Americanism'. This transcendence was additionally due to America's economic supremacy, the expansion of its film industry, and the globalised appeal of its consumer products.

Hollywood and American music became vital components of national identity and culture across the globe. Not only did they influence people's identities, but these segments of the American lifestyle created a form of impressionable regard around the world known as 'the American life'. The portrayal of freedom, opportunity, and prosperity in American media served as a driving force of the so-called 'American Dream', which eventually became known globally. Such ideas and motives heavily inspire millions of people.

American clothing brands and the new technology they manufactured became increasingly available around the globe and were considered the leading symbol of advancement and modernity. Products American manufactured were often looked at with great esteem and regarded as a symbol of affluence and unmatched quality.

Alongside its exports, the United States actively participated in setting global norms and standards. The additional intonation of the English language and its commonality in diplomacy, business, and academia helped fuel American influence by making the promotion of American ideals and values much easier.

On the other hand, the ascendance of American cultural dominance led to arguments of cultural imperialism and homogenisation. Critics argued that the one-sided promotion of American cultural exports would obliterate local culture, languages, and art traditions, leading to a single culture globally instead of celebrating diversity and heritage.

Americanism, with its transformative power, has reshaped the outlooks, hopes, and cultural identifications of societies around the globe. The dynamic relationship of soft power, economic strength, and identity projection internationally is showcased through the dissemination of American cultural elements to the rest of the world, alongside the American public.

Diplomatic Strategy: Leading the Western Bloc

The United States' diplomacy in leading the Western Bloc after the Second World War was a complex interplay of power, influence, and cooperation. When the Cold War began, the United States led the rest of the Western world in countering Soviet expansionist intentions. The US sought to integrate Soviet expansionism in Europe using economic aid, military treaties, and diplomacy to foster strong anti-communist feelings allied to US hegemony. This strategy was underpinned by the Marshall Plan, which set out to fund the post-war reconstruction of Western European countries to win their support and foster a US-aligned bloc. The formation of NATO also demonstrated the US commitment to collective defence and shared security with its Western allies. This framework was not only successful in curbing Soviet expansion but also helped further entrench American dominance in the Western bloc. Apart from military and economic superpower tactics, the US sought to exercise dominance by using soft power through cultural diplomacy through the Fulbright Programme and other educational exchange programmes.

These initiatives, in essence, sought to enforce American ideology while further solidifying the alignment of Western countries to one singular vision of democracy and freedom. At the same time, the diplomatic policy used active peace and conflict resolution strategies to settle Western disputes and preserve the unity of effort crucial in confronting the Soviet threat. The Bretton Woods Conference and its successors, like the International Monetary Fund (IMF) and the World Bank, epitomised the American attempts to construct a post-World War international economic order dominated by the Western bloc. Diplomatically, the United Nations served a different purpose and became another arena where the US sought to contain communist expansion and gain supporters for American policies and US-led initiatives. In many cases, the US took the position of mediator, builder of consensus and, in some cases, even the initiator of a series of diplomatic compromises. In other words, the diplomatic strategy to lead the Western bloc made use of US initiatives interrelated with an economically facilitated approach within the diplomatic framework of developed military alliances, cultural outreach, and multi-dimensional diplomacy to – in a unified and strong response – counter the Soviet Union's aggressive ideological assault and geopolitical expansion.

Technological Shifts: Innovations and Advances

The era after World War II ended brought with it a shift in technology that seemed to impact the world all at once. The US and the UK, with their collaborative efforts, led the way in technological advancements, particularly in aerospace and electronics, updating the dynamics of power and influence on the world stage.

The advancements in technology and their impact on aviation were of core importance. The US and the UK achieved tremendous improvements in the aviation sector, leading them to jet engines, supersonic aircraft, and space exploration. This surge in aerospace capabilities had profound implications for military dominance, strategic projection, and scientific achievement. Moreover, the collaborative efforts of the UK and the US for aerospace technology improved their diplomatic support and changed the political environment, making them prominent figures worldwide.

At the same time, this area saw the development of electronics. The development of semiconductors, transistors and later, integrated circuits gave rise to the digital world we live in today. The US and UK were leading these advances and introduced the world to telecommunications, computing, and information technology innovations. The rapid development of electronic systems enhanced military and intelligence operations, but, more importantly, changed the world from an economic and societal standpoint.

The US and UK were at the forefront of the nuclear technology race. The research, development, and use of deterrence technology were evolving at an astonishing rate. The rise of nuclear power and weapons changed the international peace and security strategy and diplomacy calculus. The technological race between the two superpowers defined the Cold War context and shifted the global balance of power.

Lastly, innovation in medical technology, agricultural practices, and industrial automation changed the standard of living and productivity. The US and UK played a major role in these developments, utilising their scientific intellect and vast knowledge from research and emerging technologies, affirming their status as major international leaders.

The international order has fundamentally changed because of the collaboration and rivalry of the US and UK regarding cutting-edge technologies. The shift in technologies had a seriously deep impact on a country's power, strategic ties with other countries, and a nation's economic dependencies.

Challenges And Cohesion In The Post-War Era

After the Second World War ended, the global landscape underwent several changes. The changes opened new challenges, opportunities, and even more unexplored possibilities. In the post-war period, numerous foreign policies came into play, and new forms of sentiments and trends emerged across nations, uniting or dividing them. Although there was the US as the dominant global superpower, the multi-faceted complexities of the world posed new challenges.

Possibly the most glaring issue reconciling the post-war period was reconstruction and recovery as Europe was in shambles. War had wreaked havoc on infrastructure, economies, and societies, and rebuilding everything from the ground up was a monumental challenge. At the same time, the decolonisation movements throughout Asia, Africa, and the Middle East presented powerful obstacles for former colonial powers trying to offer independence while maintaining their influence and self-interest within the region.

In addition, ideological battles emerged, especially at the onset of the Cold War between the United States and the Soviet Union. These two superpowers began creating a new environment of intense competition and tension. This shift in ideology not only grappled with international relations but also resulted in proxy battles in many different areas, further adding to the already complex global geopolitical scope.

These challenges all aimed to promote cohesion and international cooperation. The United Nations and other institutions were carefully crafted to increase collaboration, protect peace, and tackle some of the world's most crucial problems. Alongside them, entities like the Marshall Plan focused on advancing regions that had recently suffered from wars while supporting global stability, peace, and economic prosperity.

The establishment of military coalitions and alliances

also emerged in the same post-war period. NATO was created in 1949 precisely to provide collective defence among the Western powers, encourage cohesion, and deter potential opponents who could threaten. Also, during this time, numerous bilateral agreements and security pacts enhanced the defence architecture of the region.

There were clearly new developments in the social and cultural front areas, attributable to the fact that people began embracing the culture of the United States alongside the development of mass media, which affected the perception and identities of every region in the world. Though these social changes created opportunities for better cross-cultural communication and understanding, they also created issues regarding preserving varying cultures and heritage.

Overall, the post-war period was an area of crisis, reaction, and change. After a global conflict, nations tended to find and deal with multiple issues while attempting to maintain unity and peace in an ever-changing world order. All of these factors suggest ongoing impacts in international relations and that the post-war period is significant in regard to geopolitical influence.

Implications for Modern Power Transitions

The world's geopolitical order was largely shaped by the US and UK's power transitions after World War II. Understanding these countries is vital for modern foresight on global power relations and anticipating future trends.

They provide rich testimony of power transition phenomena and their relevance to the contemporary world.

One universal primary consequence marks changes in global leadership. After World War II, the US emerged as a dominantly powerful state, possessing unmatched economic, militaristic, and diplomatic influence over the world. The change in global leadership from Britain to American hegemony initiated the transformation of the world order to a novel international order. Global politics is largely guided by contemporary norms and institutions emanating from this era. Power transitions continue to fuel contemporary discourse on the relationship between ruling powers and emerging contending forces.

In addition, the case of the US and the UK illustrates the blending of economic, military, and cultural factors about power change. A new Bretton Woods system was established after the Second World War under the leadership of the US to stabilise and recover Europe economically. In contrast, the decline of the British Empire illustrates the deep relationship between economics and a country's global standing. This blend of economic power and dynamic influence continues to be relevant in studying the emergence of new international actors like China and their role in shaping the existing balance of power.

"It also draws attention to the timeless US-UK special relationship in the context of bilateral international relations after the US-dominated British hegemonic influence, showing the importance of relationships and alliances during a time of power change."

With all these changes, perhaps the most important

lesson from US-UK bilateral relations is the importance of building strategic relationships and maintaining partnerships to preserve global stability while addressing emerging shared challenges.

Ultimately, the consequences derived from analysing the power shifts of the US and UK are pivotal in understanding contemporary international relations. A careful analysis of these transitions provides crucial insights regarding the essence of power, the processes of its transitions, and the implications of such changes within the context of global governance. With the rise of new regions of global influence and the transformation of traditional spheres of power, the case of US and UK relations stands as a model for decision-makers, researchers, and activists interested in the intricacies of contemporary power transitions.

6

A Contemporary Analysis
The Rise of China

Historical Context and Modern Implications

The developments in China during the late 20th century were foundational in transforming the current contemporary landscape of China's position in the world. The death of Mao Zedong heralded a new phase of reforms in China that radically transformed China's economy, politics, and social structure. With the adoption of the "opening up and reform" policy by Deng Xiaoping, China experienced a new era of engagement with international markets and investment. This fundamental change set the trend for industrialisation, urbanisation, and technological advancement, which led to China emerging as a global economic superpower. China, the most populous country in the world, also faced myriad sociopolitical challenges that required careful management of a sense of communism alongside emerging capitalist forces. Adopting socialism with Chinese characteristics transformed domestic policies and strategies and fundamentally altered the entire approach to global policies and power relations.

The historical account of China's modernisation intertwines with various events, particularly its membership in the World Trade Organization in 2001. This milestone exposed China to tremendous opportunities alongside exposure to new challenges. The subsequent increase in foreign direct investment, trade, and technological exchanges profoundly altered China's position in the global economy. The 2013 Belt and Road Initiative (BRI) exemplifies China's aggressive efforts to increase geopolitical and infrastructural influence. The BRI is not merely an economic initiative but also represents a shift in strategic global dynamics, illustrating China's ambition to reshape its role on the world stage. Furthermore, as a reminder of the Silk Road, it reflects China's contemporary resurgence of historically inspired focus on expansive trade routes and other intercontinental networks.

The convergence of these historical turning points has given China's global significance a distinctive twist. Appealing to the frameworks of history, it is essential to assess modern China's rise in power in the context of the multipolar world. This study examines the changes and consequences brought about by China's resurgence, including changes in its role as a world power, diplomatic relations, and the global and regional equilibrium shift. Understanding the context of the past and juxtaposing it with the present enables a profoundly accurate analysis of China's surge and helps determine its features on the global stage. This evaluation is crucial for understanding China's historical progress during the evolution of the global system. It is essential to explore the forces behind its current state while tracing its historical timeline.

Political Landscape: Communism, Governance, and Leadership

Regarding China's current political situation, the development and adaptation of communism into the Chinese system has remained one of the most crucial factors. Concerning the ideologies of communism, China can trace its historical roots back to its fundamental leader, Mao Zedong, and his policies that eventually led to the emergence of the communist state in 1949. The later formal adoption of power by the Chinese Communist Party, the CCP, has undergone a transformation in the governance system where power is integrated and monopolised by the Party, systematising the most critical aspect of control and command capitalism, which is the central decision and authority of the CCP. The Party is the most dominant control exercised over the government, policies, economy, and social life. To operate this way, the Party has to 'manage' the ICP by ensuring that each member follows the basic rules of discipline, organisation propaganda techniques, and control of concepts featuring counter quasi-opposition movements targeted against efforts to transform development into socialism with Chinese characteristics. Another phenomenon impacting the country's political system is collective leadership, where executive authority shifts among several leaders selected for that purpose. The policymaking processes are more the result of bargaining among senior Party members instead of rational choice, with changes in society's norms made over time. The leadership in the CCP is of paramount importance since these structures are built on rotation systems, meaning that the promotion system is partly based on performance, thereby making the policies and guidelines easier to follow and making it simpler for loyal members - if they so wish - to adhere to the policies and guidelines set forth by the leadership.

The connection between political ideology and practical policies has always persisted in the governance of China as it attempts to solve domestic and international problems. The term 'socialist democracy' attempts to capture the essence of the one-party system that blends communism with some degree of participation by the people in decision-making processes, allowing the Party to maintain its primary control as it is the one that makes the fundamental decisions. A comprehensive understanding of China's political system requires examining the construct of its governance system under communist ideology and the nature of its leadership cum politics. It is clear that as China's international prominence increases, these political elements become important factors to consider regarding the direction the country will take, its development, and its relationships with other countries in the world.

Economic Growth and Global Influence

The extraordinary growth of China's economy in the past few decades has not only propelled the nation into one of the most powerful economies in the world but also significantly transformed the global economic landscape. The shift from a planned economy to a more market-oriented one has driven China's export objectives, leading the government to actively promote its economic infrastructure and system. This proactive approach has enhanced international trade by opening up its markets worldwide for various products, including exports in consumer electronics, textiles, heavy machinery, and high-tech products, thereby reshaping global trade dynamics.

This rapid expansion of the economy has not only made China a global economic powerhouse but also provided the means to offer economic aid and invest in many nations across the globe, thereby transforming the social structure of economic relations globally. Initiatives like the Belt and Road Initiative, a strategic move to improve cooperation and connectivity between Asia, Africa, and Europe, have allowed China to assert its gainful political and economic control over the region. The Belt and Road Initiative, which encompasses a series of large-scale infrastructure programmes, has not only improved trade, transportation, and economic growth for the neighbouring countries and China but also created stronger economic ties, thereby enhancing China's geopolitical influence.

In addition, China's participation in global investment streams such as the Asian Infrastructure Investment Bank (AIIB) marks a significant change in global finance and the development of new monetary systems. The greater use of the Chinese currency in international trade transactions is a clear evidence of the efforts of the People's Republic to expand its influence in the world monetary system. By increasing the value of the country's currency in international transactions, China is not only improving its own economy but also reducing the value of American financial systems, thereby fueling debates over the global economic framework and highlighting the far-reaching implications of China's financial strategies.

China's innovation, technology, and research investments increase its global relationships and standing. The country's rapid advancements in artificial intelligence, quantum computing, renewable energy, and aerospace technology have made China a leading competitor in the global technology race. With so much money put into research and development and industry captures that are strategically bought out, Chinese companies have risen to dominate the emerging industries and change the nature of competition while raising concerns about protecting intellectual property and competition practices.

In addition, China's active participation in several forums and governance systems demonstrates the country's willingness to participate in formulating and implementing international economic policies. China is positioning itself to construct and dominate the discussions for policy-setting on economic governance by defending inclusive globalisation, sustainable development, and climate change initiatives while redefining a multipolar world order.

Technological Advancements and Innovations

The technological advancements and innovations being pursued within China have garnered significant attention on the global stage. With substantial investments in research and development, China has made remarkable strides in various technology sectors like artificial intelligence, quantum computing, biotechnology, and even renewable energy. Under its strategies, China is focusing on achieving technological self-sufficiency, thus switching its emphasis to more self-dependent initiatives. It aims to attain dominance in specific industries and decrease reliance on foreign technologies.

China is trying to broaden its horizons and be at the forefront of everything within the artificial intelligence industry. With financial support, government policies, and funding, AI research centres and companies have developed, leading to breakthroughs in machine learning, computer vision, and natural language processing. These changes helped fuel innovation in the country while allowing China to advance as a global AI market competitor.

China's efforts in technological innovation also apply to many emerging fields, such as quantum computing. The country has financed a considerable amount of quantum research to tap into the powerful computational ability that quantum systems can provide. Such advancement may result in changes in cryptography, materials science, and optimisation, altering the technological world order.

Another area of focus for Chinese development is biotechnology and pharmaceuticals, which are accelerating rapidly. Merged areas of research, such as genetics, personalised medicine, and biopharmaceutical manufacturing, place China at the centre of activity in this crucial area. Focus on healthcare genomics, bioinformatics, precision medicine, and other enabling medicines indicates that China seeks to make powerful discoveries in science and technology while also solving important healthcare problems.

Also, China's contemplations on sustainable energy have helped It make great strides in revolutionising energy technologies. China has also enhanced its use of renewable resources like solar, wind, and advanced energy systems to fight climate change and achieve energy independence. Development in infrastructure and clean energy projects showcases the country's determination to emerge as a green and sustainable development race leader.

To sum up, the cultivated level of new and advanced technology infrastructures China has attained in different economic sectors hopefully indicates the country's aim of securing leadership in the globe's socio-economic competitions. The changes and advancements in technological infrastructure are expected to alter global balance, competition, and industry – it becomes clear that studying China's technological innovation provides an understanding of the country's changing position on the world stage.

Military Development and Strategic Posturing

Experts and global security analysts have focused on accelerating China's military capabilities in the past few years. The pace at which its defence systems are being modernised and its military infrastructure expanded is a concerning factor for international relations and the balance of power in the region. China is considered to be emerging as a military power, especially in the Asia-Pacific region, due to its vast and growing navy, air force, missile defence systems, and the world's largest army.

A distinctive feature of China's military strategy is its focus on A2/AD and asymmetric warfare. Maximising an offensive and defence strategy helps neutralise a potential threat or enemy. China aims to avert counter-regional power actions by developing A2/AD and anti-ship ballistic missiles, expanding the fleet of submarines, and building advanced cyber warfare technologies.

Moreover, China's southward and eastward expansion into the South China Sea and East China Sea has caused disputes regarding sovereignty with other countries, which has received the concern of the United States alongside other world powers. China's construction of military bases and facilities on artificial islands, as well as the creation of Air Defence Identification Zones (ADIZ), indicates a large degree of expansion of China's military overreach, which poses a question regarding its international obligations and compliance with global laws and agreements.

For its part in expanding military infrastructure, China is actively engaging in military modernisation programmes and developing advanced technologies, including hypersonic weapons, quantum computing, and space dominion. These improvements strengthen the traditional branches of the Chinese armed forces and profoundly affect the prospects for future wars, transforming the landscape of 21st-century warfare.

The world watches closely how China's military activities and growth affect the region's security balance. China traditionally claims its military postures are defensive, aimed at protecting national sovereignty and defending its territory. Nevertheless, the speed and volume of its military developments are continuously recalibrating geopolitical calculations and changing the Indo-Pacific defence policies. Stakeholders must develop approaches to address the gaps in constructive dialogue and build trust in the pace of China's military advancement to reduce the risk of miscalculation and ensure peaceful coexistence amid fluctuating security complexities.

Cultural Diplomacy and Soft Power

Soft Power and cultural diplomacy, as demonstrated by

China, are pivotal in shaping a nation's foreign influence and international relations. China's strategic use of its rich culture, practices, artwork, literature, traditions, and contemporary works like musical art has not only promoted China as an economic and cultural powerhouse but also fostered global understanding and cooperation. The establishment of Confucius Institutes, Chinese language programmes, and traditional cultural exchanges with numerous countries has expanded China's diplomatic reach, positioning it as a beacon of advanced culture. These efforts transcend mere political or economic alliances, paving the way for a more harmonious global community.

Moreover, the increasing acceptance and consumption of Chinese films, music, and television series serve to project China's self-image and promote multiculturalism and nationalism. Benevolence and Harmony, some of the key principles of Confucianism, are promoted through culture, which in turn helps shape and improve foreign perceptions of China.

In addition to employing traditional culture, China has leveraged soft power through new IT media technologies such as mobile applications and social media to digitally strengthen its influence internationally. China has established a presence in the virtual realm alongside arts and culture, technological innovation, and social achievement. Such achievements open avenues for the nation to share its values, engage with the world, and extend cultural exchange.

However, alongside expanding soft power presence, China has to face potential criticism and challenges.

Controversies revolving around censorship, human rights, and differing ideologies continue having an impact on China's power. This power has to censor diplomacy and involves different perspectives in order to achieve humanitarian balance in policies away from the one-sided approach in international relations. These challenges, while not insurmountable, do present significant hurdles that China must navigate in its quest for global influence.

This underscores the application of cultural public relations, and all other relations associated in the country and abroad, to showcase soft power and influence. Some central regions are universally appreciated in order to steer a narrative. By employing heritage as well as its modernisation, it seeks and enables dialogue for understanding and collaboration sharpened to strengthen approaches to building a multipolar world.

Social Issues and Development Challenges In China

China's social issues are directly related to its development challenges. Along with rapid growth in economic and global diversification, the world's most populous nation is also facing an overwhelming number of internal issues.

The unprecedented transformation in China over the past few decades has brought about a structural shift in its society, presenting both opportunities and risks for governance and stability. The government is confronted with the daunting task of managing the conflict between rural and urban societies, which often lack the necessary standards for education, healthcare, and other social amenities. This struggle underscores the immense challenges China faces in ensuring social equality and harmony, evoking a sense of empathy for the complexities of governance.

On top of that, China has to contend with issues particularly concerning the raising of children that are increasing in age along with disparities within governance arising from previous policies such as the one-child policy. From allocating sparse benefits and ensuring a healthy social support network to managing population sustainability, this shift in demography poses some complex policy hurdles, especially juggling policies towards social security systems or a steady workforce. Growth within the economy and maintaining ideological controls is a balancing act the government still grapples with, trying to stimulate invention and entrepreneurship while keeping social control.

As a result of ongoing modernisation and urbanisation, social dynamics in China have become increasingly sophisticated due to the interplay of cultural differences and generational changes. One of the most revealing aspects is that the younger generation has distinct, ever-changing ambitions and desires, many of which are shaped by international culture and technology. These shifts can create new pathways for societal renewal but can also pose conflicts where traditional values clash with modernistic thinking.

At the same time, the integration of Chinese society with the digital realm creates additional challenges for the management of public discourse and information censorship. The emergence of social media and other digital platforms has reduced communication to sound bites, which, in turn, influences public opinion and social harmony. Striking a balance between leveraging the benefits of digital connectivity and resolving privacy, misinformation, and cyber-security issues is a challenge that policymakers need to address. Moreover, the interplay of traditional values and modernistic thinking can lead to conflicts in societal renewal, as the younger generation's changing ambitions and desires may clash with established norms and values.

Amidst these complex domestic challenges and social dynamics, the Chinese government aims to foster a harmonious and socially stable society by levelling inequality while tackling the mosaic nature of its populations. It is vital to manage these challenges effectively for China to endure changes in society and its positioning in the world.

Environmental Policies and Global Developments Concerns

With the current environmental changes, China's global environmental policies have come under deep examination and concern. Air and water pollution, deforestation, and the depletion of biodiversity have become severe issues for China as it transforms its economy. To comprehensively deal with resource depletion, the state has set ambitious policies aimed at improving the environment. China has made and continues to make vast progress in adopting greener technologies and sustainable practices. It is now the world's largest investor in renewable energy sources and is steering towards decreasing its carbon emissions. Furthermore, China's involvement in international environmental treaties and agreements demonstrates its willingness to address global issues.

The Belt and Road Initiative (BRI) has the potential to improve, as well as weaken, the environmental policies of China. It has been observed that the BRI could serve as a way for China to gain geopolitical and economic leverage but that the programme could also expand its carbon footprint and infrastructure. The BRI, with its extensive infrastructure projects, could significantly impact the environment, both positively and negatively. China must carefully balance its economic and geopolitical interests with its environmental responsibilities when implementing BRI projects.

China's active participation in collaborative efforts is instrumental in addressing global environmental issues. By working with other countries and organisations, China is leveraging its power and resources to foster international environmental programmes. This proactive stance reassures the audience about the collective efforts being made to combat environmental challenges.

Encouraging sustainable practices within the country and promoting them outside strengthens China's perception as a responsible member of the international community. Such efforts accompany the goals of conservation and climate adaptation and emphasise China's dedication to international environmental policies.

While crafting its strategies on the environment, international obligations, and other policies, China has to deal with tricky situations like balancing its economy with environmental protection, making friends internationally while nurturing its own policies, and protecting the country's sovereignty. China's policy decisions will shape much of the world's progress on environmental issues, and it will need to adapt swiftly to better-aligned strategies.

The Belt and Road Initiative: Expanding Reach

In 2013, President Xi Jinping of China proposed the Belt and Road Initiative (BRI), an unprecedented strategy aimed at developing economic and infrastructure relations in countries along the ancient Silk Road. Xi envisioned bridging physical infrastructure like highways, railways, and ports, integrating digital systems, finance, and social relations with the Chinese heart, thus creating international value chains. Over 140 countries and international organisations have expressed their support for the BRI. This underlines why China's BRI is deemed critical not only for its economic benefits but also for global geopolitics, diplomacy, and economy.

At its core, the BRI envisages mutual benefit from increased trade and cultural interaction among nations, transcontinentally on an unprecedented scale. China attempts to achieve its regional and global development goals via trade. As seen, The Belt and Road Initiative intends to create paths and opportunities for fostering trade and investment to generate comprehensive benefits more accessible to all societies. Expanding sustainable development has been given due attention while striving to expand the project scope. Other commitments made by China within the BRI framework regarding the green agenda indicators include ensuring ecological safety standards.

Nonetheless, the BRI has encountered scrutiny and criticism, with some raising concerns about the impact on financial sustainability, transparency, the environment, and geopolitical intentions. Detractors argue that some BRI projects may create a dependency on debt for the participating countries, possibly jeopardising their autonomy. Also, doubts have been raised regarding aligning BRI projects with local exigencies and the environmental impacts, highlighting the need for responsible and sustainable action.

As the BRI broadens its scope, it can transform geopolitical relations and realign economic relationships in different regions. Its effectiveness will rely on the focus brought to managing risks and challenges and incorporating the diverse views and interests of the countries involved. The BRI presents an unparalleled chance to enhance and deepen discussion, understanding, and cooperation between the countries that go beyond the conventional hurdles, stimulating the nurturing of a collective future. Within the context of international relations, understanding this initiative, which is highly complex and possibly multifaceted, will assist in comprehending contemporary evolving international relations, especially in the 21st century.

Managing Relations of the US with China in the 21st Century

In the twenty-first century, the relationship that the United States holds with China has further developed into one of the most crucial and multi-layered themes that pose challenges to the balance of global stability, as well as to the socio-economic progress of the world. Of paramount concern is that they are very influential at this particular moment, making their connections and cooperations a global watch. US-China relations are characterised by deep economic interdependence, geopolitical rivalry, ideological differences, and some levels of strategic cooperation. This part analyses the intricacies of this relationship and seeks the ways that are helpful to reduce problems and constructive conflicts.

Economic Interdependence: The relationship between the United States and China is one of the most complex and developed interrelations, as they are vital economies for one another. The commercial relations and flows of investments as well as the linkage of the supply chains shows their deep-rooted interdependence relations. But at the same time, there are trade disputes, issues of intellectual property rights, and even barriers to entering the market, which have damaged the economic ties between them. The imposition of tariffs and other trade barriers has emerged from conflicting negotiations of these countries' mutually advantageous and equitable trade policies. In case there is an initiative to negotiate the fair and balanced terms free of trade conflicts and structural discriminatory obstacles, cooperation initiatives will be developed.

Geopolitical Competition: The United States and China compete on multiple fronts as part of international rivalry, particularly in the Asia Pacific region. Complications over territorial disputes, military activities, and alliances continue to fuel strategic competitions that worsen security dilemmas and military posturing. Increasing strategic distrust makes promoting understanding and stability difficult. Diplomacy and multilateralism are instrumental in managing differences, increasing the level of openness, and preventing actions that risk escalating tensions regarding regional and global security.

Ideological Disparities: The US has complicated relations with China due to the ideological differences between the two nations. Differences in governance and the existence of human rights and democracy create diplomatic friction not only for policy formulation but also for discourse. Protecting interests and crafting a constructive working partnership require focusing on joint aims, albeit some differences need acceptance. Bridging an ideological gap entails open discussions on differences and acknowledging common interests.

Strategic Cooperation: Despite the difficulties, there are opportunities for strategic cooperation between the

U.S. and China. Combating climate change, non-proliferation, public health, and scientific research are all important areas in which both nations and the global community would benefit from collaboration. When developed and cultivated, these spheres of cooperation promote the building of trust, conflict resolution, and stability in international relations.

Conclusion: Diplomacy, well-planned policies, and ongoing negotiations are critical in addressing the complex dynamics of US and China relations. The intertwining factors of competition and collaboration, in addition to the ever-growing divergence of interests, are challenges to be dealt with by both sides. A profound understanding that recognising complexities, shouldering responsibilities, and drawing distinctions is vital to a constructive approach to these relations in the 21st century.

7

Economic Competitions
Trade and Technological Supremacy

Economic Power Dynamics: An Overview

The relationship between a country's economy and political power, both domestically and internationally, is asymmetric and has major impacts on various aspects of the world. No single international problem can be resolved without considering the economy and geopolitical situation. Over the past few decades, the world has witnessed unprecedented shifting patterns of global economic activity. Today's most visible phenomenon is the transformation of economies of developing countries such as China, India, Brazil, and others. While the once unmoving economic giants, namely the United States, European Union, and Japan, are transforming their faces to adjust to the new markets and opportunities available, it is equally important that the competing nations have 'battle-hardened' themselves for the adjustments. This chapter shall analyse the basic contours and characteristics of the ever-evolving relationships of power that characterise trade, investment, innovation, and resources.

The complex structure of trade relations linking countries internationally lies at the core of the trade dynamics. The growth of globalisation is fuelling the interdependence of economies, which hastens the movement of goods, services, and money across borders. Trade has always been a key activity in the development and growth of the economy. However, the new developments and patterns of trade, the new agreements, and trade blocs have made many changes that are difficult to understand in relations of dominance and control between countries. In addition, the competition in the market, coupled with the integration of new technology, supply chain management, and marketing, has changed the competition level, r, resulting in more intense competition and new strategic direction.

As mentioned, trade is not the only thing that links economic power with actual power. One of the more recent and innovative sources of economic power is the ability to invent something new or create new technologies. That is why the ability to create new technologies, enforce patent rights, and restructure an economy makes someone an economic power. Different countries compete to dominate in artificial intelligence, renewable energy, biotechnology, and other spheres like cyber security, which shows that domination in technological spheres is one major power and influence in international relations. As noted, the competition for technological power has produced, on the one hand, partnerships and friendly coalitions and, on the other hand, competitors who motivate each other inside coalitions that are formed through diplomatic processes or negotiations.

In addition, the control of financial resources, currency value, and market operations falls under economic power dynamics. All the elaborate steps constituting economic power, including the movement of exchange rates, the strategy of tax policy, and the control of financial institutions, are integrated into the changeable manoeuvres of fiscal authority. Understanding how such interconnections affect local economies and global market systems is pivotal to understanding the power of states and regions in the international economic system.

As the focus of economic power dynamics shifts continuously, policy of the state, international corporations, and the resurgence of economic nationalism forms a vital point of intersect. Economic nationalism, a doctrine that emphasises the importance of domestic control over the economy, is gaining traction in certain circles. Southern governments exercise their power over international trade and investment-setting tariffs, regulating foreign direct investment, and formulating industrial policy. These policies are paralleled with the activities and conduct of international companies. At the same time, the revival of economic nationalism in certain circles complexifies profoundly the established structures of economic power relations and the norms of economic might and affluence.

The Evolution of Trade Relations

The evolution of trade relations shows the barter systems of ancient civilisations to the establishment of formalised networks for commerce. Trade relations have long served as a backbone for the economic interaction of different nations which has eased international relations and enhanced their growth. Trade relations have improved and enhanced due to the proliferation of the Silk Ripple, a historical trade route that connected the East and the West, the maritime trade of spices, and the movement of culture, goods and even ideas through continents. During the era of colonialism, with increased prowess in navigation and technological growth, western powers were able to dominate the world through trade, which biased the economic transition further. The industrial revolution enabled trade relations to execute globally due to mass production of goods and the formation of new markets as a result of overexploitation.

The onset of globalisation marked a new phase in trade relations due to increased interdependence. The establishment of international organisations like the World Trade Organisation (WTO) aimed to consolidate global trade, foster cooperation, and reduce trade barriers. This resulted in the creation of multinational companies and the integration of supply chains on an international level, which radically changed the face of trade relations. Moreover, technological advancement and the growth of communication networks changed the trade process by making it easier to conduct real-time transactions and cross-border investments.

In the past few decades, the economic and political transformations of emerging markets have reshaped the lines of trade, underscoring the urgency and significance of these changes. The rise of China as an emerging economic giant has shifted the world's economic debate towards fair competition, intellectual property rights, and access to markets. At the same time, the traditional boundaries were overwhelmed by the rapid development of digital trade and e-commerce, altering the attitude of consumers and business activities; automation and lack of regulations created new problems and opportunities on the borders of trade relations.

Projections foreshadow that relations between countries will be impacted by innovation and sustainability, as well as changes in the global power structure. The protective measures taken in various regions, along with the digital revolution, highlight the need for foreign trades to be remodelled. Countries are expected to tackle issues of ethical trading, environmental policies, and labour measures that will encourage the fostering of trade in the 21st century. The importance of these issues in shaping the future of trade cannot be overstated, and their effective management will be key to fostering healthy and sustainable trade relations.

Tech Race: Innovation as a Battlefield

Countries worldwide are competing to achieve global dominance. The 21st century is forecasted to be full of powerful rivalries that will transform the world into a more competitive arena. Such rivalry, referred to as a 'tech race,' emphasises the need to continuously innovate and resort to technological upgrades. A competition of this sort not only raises the stakes economically but also poses a threat to national security, intellectual property, and diplomacy.

The focus of the frantic race towards modernisation is attaining supremacy in core domains, including artificial intelligence, quantum computing, biotechnology, and advanced manufacturing. To capture these base-shifting technologies, countries pour funds into R&D, collaborate with the academic and business sectors, and develop elaborate national policies and plans. Militarily, countries aim to conquer as many technologies as possible due to the obvious economic benefits and the significant strategic and geopolitical implications that arise from it.

Moreover, competition within this rise in technology is multi-dimensional, involving a fusion of civilian and military sectors, further straining the division between sectors and realms. The overlap of advanced technologies with military capabilities has stimulated new forms of competition, resulting in fears of arms races in cyberspace and space, where innovation poses great danger and risk towards national security and international stability.

In addition, the race for dominance in these nascent technologies is compounding the struggle to create standards and norms that will determine the future of global technology. The debate around the privacy of information, protection of data, and the ethics of using technology under development reveals the competitiveness of this context, as countries compete to control the regulatory environment for the application and dissemination of transformational technologies.

With the tech race being as aggressive as it is, creating responsible and collaborative standards of behaviour will effectively address the non-cooperative side of the race while also focusing on societal benefit and progress. Ensuring that a technological race becomes a race that yields benefits to all humanity, rather than fostering further fragmentation and discord, requires that sovereign states balance competition with cooperation, foster healthy debate, and jointly address existing global issues.

Intellectual Property and Its Global Implications

Recently, the role of 'intellectual property' (IP) is increasingly becoming the backbone of a country's economic development and technological progress. Protection of assets, including Patents, Trademarks, Service marks, Copyrights, and Trade secrets, impacts business and economic development on a global scale. At the global level, the challenge of international competition has intensified on all fronts, and with it, the enforcement and IP infringement problems have taken centre stage. Unauthorised usage or duplication of proprietary inventions can diminish the possessor's competitive edge, as well as create a harmful impact on global trade, competition, and innovation. The specific area of IP and its consequences on the world economy is very deep in scope. The first one is the significance of IP as a catalyst for innovation and investment in research and development. By looking at the case studies of top IP innovators from different countries, we understand the importance of effective IP enforcement policies and how this results in sustainable technological development. Also, this part deals with the impact of enforcement of IP rights and the difficulties involved in it in the context of international trade and globalisation.

The increasing instances of counterfeiting and cyber theft have prompted the alignment of IP regulations towards standardisation and enhanced integration in primary sectors of the economy. Also, the relationship between competition within the market and the IP market tends to indicate that fostering competition balanced with incentivising innovation is fundamental. Current analysis of case laws and judicial decisions challenges how intellectual property protection interfaces with antitrust and competition legislation. The consequences of IPs' differing standards and policies are analysed in this area of at least two jurisdictions with bilateral or multilateral treaties. Unifying intellectual property policies contribute more to lowering entry barriers for business and competition on the global market. Hence, policies designed to defend, transfer, and exploit international property in a knowledge-based economy would require this understanding for sustainable economic growth and development.

Supply Chains and Market Dependencies

Nowadays, modern supply chains, which play an integral part in the global economy, impact market dependency and international relations. The web of providers, producers, and sellers has created an unheard-of level of dependence among countries, and this interdependence grows with increased trade. The analysis covers the complex structures of supply chains and their effects on market dependencies and international relations. This will conclude with a subsection on trade dynamics, focusing on the geopolitical aspects of trade policies and attempts at international market integration from a supply-side perspective.

The modern supply chain goes beyond national borders and encompasses the whole economy and society, comprising raw material suppliers, production facilities, transportation, and distribution systems. Trade between nations evidences their dependence on each other to obtain critical components and principal goods. This creates a delicate balance of power where nations depend on certain countries or regions to provide vital resources and products. If these resources are disrupted, the powers shift, and the effects such disruptions can have on multiple economies and industries can be catastrophic.

In addition, the use of modern technologies has reshaped the management of supply chains, allowing for the monitoring of movements in real-time, improving operational productivity, and implementing just-in-time delivery systems. The deeper level of interaction has also presented issues associated with cybersecurity and information privacy as supply chains become more reliant on digital systems. There are additional challenges to achieving resilience and security because cyber threats to interconnected supply chains are easily vulnerable.

The dependencies of a market have an intimate relationship with the level of balance and continuity of control of the supply chains. Changes in trade policy, like tariffs and even geopolitical matters, can shift the market, alter supplier loyalty, and create marketplace exposure. Understanding these dynamics is important to developing sound economic policies with less probability of possible damage.

In addition, the COVID-19 pandemic exposed the weaknesses in global supply chains. Disruptions in one part of the world caused a ripple effect that led to shortages and problems in entire regions and a broad spectrum of industries. This emphasises the need to strengthen the capability to withstand unanticipated disruption by increasing the diversity of supply sources and improving domestic production capacity broadly.

The construction of economic and trade relations geared towards supply chains fostering goodwill and reciprocity is crucial as countries try to cope with the complexities of interdependencies. Supply chains can be strengthened through cooperation in tackling common challenges, including sustainability, ethical sourcing, and fairness in labour practices.

To sum up, the complex relationship between market dependencies and supply chains highlights the interrelated nature of the world economy. Considering the effects of market dependencies and managing supply chains coherently is important for dealing with the challenges characterising international economic relations' horizon.

Currency Influences and Financial Markets

Financial markets and currency are the backbone of international relations and play a pivotal role in global economic power play. The valuation and policy surrounding a country's currency jurisdiction significantly influence trade balance, investment volume, and national power. Understanding the multidimensional relationship between currencies and financial markets is crucial for dissecting contemporary economic conflicts.

International exchange has become a basic part of human life, where exchange rate changes affect a country's ability to import and export goods, services, and capital. A devaluation of currency helps boost exports as they become cheaper; however, less imported currency strength has advantages with greater self-funding powers. On the other hand, value regression has negative effects on government controls. Such trends create capabilities for cross-border income and expenditure flow, which affect the expansion of net profits. Therefore, managing currency risks has become strategic and necessary for these organisations.

Capital markets and foreign exchange (Forex) markets are among the vital components of the international economy. Like every other market, the Forex market has a real-time trading platform for buying and selling currencies. The constant activity in a market revolves around supply, demand, and further economic progress indicators. The action of the capital markets is complementary as they allow a country to collect funds for development projects while simultaneously attracting investments in various classes to stimulate the economy and fund innovation. The reliance of the various markets on one another increases their sensitivity to the impacts of policy changes and geopolitical happenings, thus making the effects go beyond borders.

Authorities of the region, such as government institutions and central banks, have the most impact on the currency system and its financial stability. Using monetary policy, the central banks utilise options like adjusting the interest rate, employing quantitative easing policies, and other inflation-controlling factors. In addition to that, fiscal policies defined as spending, tax collection, budget compilation, and other strategies employed by the government also shape the attitude of participants in the market. Attempts to unify the approaches to policy frameworks and set guidelines for minimising systemic risks are also pursued within multilateral forums like the IMF and World Bank.

The intricate interplay of a currency's power, financial markets, and the underlying economy underscores the necessity for proactive and flexible strategies among policymakers, businesses, and investors. Achieving sustainable growth on a global scale hinges on cooperative foresight in understanding and managing the complexities of global finances and international relations.

Role of Multinational Corporations in Geopolitics

Multinational corporations (MNCs) have massively shaped the geopolitical sphere because of their ability to control international relations and the global market. They singlehandedly pull the economy up because of their operations in different countries, giving the MNCs opportunities to open a new business or invest in another. With their businesses located globally, these companies can exploit varying regulations, gaining from market differences. Because of their enormous wealth, business reach, and powerful dominion over industries, MNCs are becoming greater to develop the economy and control political and global policies.

In geopolitics, multinational corporations (MNCs) have positive and negative implications for cooperation among nations. Through carefully selecting alliances with governments and other organisations, they can aid in establishing diplomatic relations, furthering the interests of those countries and thereby strengthening global cooperation. On the other hand, their attempts to obtain favourable agreements related to trade and other administrative policies may put them in conflict with local industries and provoke national governments into adopting protectionist policies, which worsen geopolitical tensions.

Furthermore, MNCs' participation in the information technology, energy, and infrastructure sectors allows them to alter the existing power and security equilibrium state. The market control of vital resources and sophisticated technologies by these corporations can influence the global marketing of capabilities and may give rise to adversarial relations between states. It is, therefore, MNCs and national governments that, in this case, engage in the most intense struggles to control the formation of strategies and coalitions. This potential for conflict underscores the gravity of the situation and the need for careful management.

In addition, MNCs' very transnational characteristics assist them in bypassing the more state-centric boundaries to interact with different stakeholders worldwide. From this vantage point, MNCs can construct narratives, shape public perception, and advance policies that change the fundamental contours of power and control, thereby redefining the concepts of sovereignty and autonomy. Therefore, the convergence of MNCs' interests with opposing national objectives brings about often contending power structures with complex consequences for international relations.

As stated above, MNCs are a part of international trading and investment flows and constitute an important factor in geopolitics. Their activities tend to have a cross-border effect, making their contribution to international geopolitics complex while also warranting further investigation into MNCs as an asset for advancement in international economic development. The profound influence of MNCs in economics and global affairs poses threats that require clear policies to be formulated. The necessity of action to address these threats is clear, and understanding the relationship between MNCs and geopolitical factors is crucial to adapting to changes in international relations. A successful policy aimed at conflict-free cooperation will depend on this comprehension.

Government Policies and Economic Nationalism

Economic nationalism has come into sharper focus with growing geopolitical tensions and dominant countries competing with each other in an increasingly globalised world. Policies concerning trade, investment, and industrial development must be reconsidered to protect one's interests. In this context, it would be prudent to study the consequences of state policies along with economic nationalism.

Strategic industries include rapidly developing technologies, defence, and critical infrastructure that governments give primary attention to for specific development and protection. Many countries have attempted to achieve self-reliance and resilience, leading them to implement policies to limit foreign sourcing, particularly in critical domains such as energy, food security, and healthcare.

Equally important are tariff policies intended to correct actual or perceived inequities within an economy. Nations are restructuring trade relations using tariffs and trade barriers, especially to protect domestic producers and meet certain strategic goals. The shift toward protectionism is a break from established norms of free trade and globalisation and has serious consequences for the entire world economy.

Economic nationalism also covers a range of monetary policies, including the currency policies of a state that seek to maximise its exports, create competitive edges, and influence exchange rates. These actions can lead to currency conflict and the disruption of international monetary systems, which must be balanced through careful diplomacy and collaboration to minimise harm.

Government policies in collaboration with economic nationalism also include regulations on foreign direct capital investments and the enforcement of patents. Countries are imposing more restrictive policies to protect important technological and data-related advancements while monitoring the stock of foreign capital for underlying national security threats. Such policies are meant to safeguard the scope of local resources and avoid the risk of technological subsidisation or appropriation by foreign countries.

Moreover, economic nationalism is influenced by sociopolitical factors, as the public and voters dictate government actions. Economic issues usually align with nationalistic sentiments, further complicating policies and unilateral diplomacy by striking twenty birds with a single stone. The intertwining of domestic politics with economically driven solutions shifts the focus to the peculiar relationships in state policies and relevant geostrategic considerations.

The intricate web of government policy and economic nationalism requires skilful leadership, diplomacy, and international collaboration. Resolving the conflicts of national interests with globalisation requires policymakers to think of holistic approaches that enable long-term prosperity and equitable economic relationships. The imprint of government policies, along with economic nationalism, will be felt regionally and internationally for some time to come, which makes policy formulation and its subsequent implementation a matter of consequence.

Partnerships and Alliances: Shaping the Future

In an era defined by economic interdependence and geopolitical rivalry, the role of partnerships and alliances is crucial in shaping the future of global economic dynamics. As nations navigate the complexities of trade relations and technological advancements, strategic collaborations become imperative for achieving mutual prosperity and stability. Because of the multifaceted nature of partnerships and alliances, we need to shed light on their significance in addressing the challenges posed by economic competitions and fostering sustainable growth.

Effective partnerships create a knowledge-based economy that strengthens trade resilience and knowledge and resources, allowing for efficiency in productivity and enhanced trade opportunities. Strategic partnerships enable the creation of international benchmarks for best practices, policies, norms, and rules, which enhance sustainable economic synergies and reduce risks in trade.

Strategic partnerships greatly affect economic development. Nations can direct funding and investment towards infrastructure, education, and sustainable measures through these collaborative partnerships.

Countries can work together to lessen the negative effects of economic disruptions and invest in financial systems, leading to a balanced economy worldwide.

The evolving context of global economic competition brings to light the significance of mergers and alliances for addressing major global issues. Collaborative approaches are needed for solving problems like climate change, environmental conservation, and resource allocation. Nations can work together towards developing sustainable solutions using joint research, technology grants, and policy collaborations that solve environmental problems and create a green economic environment. Additionally, strategic alliances are important in addressing issues that cut across borders, such as hacking, thus helping protect the digital economy and other economic infrastructures from cyber threats.

Furthermore, mergers and alliances assist in devising diplomatic strategies for managing crises and conflicts. These partnerships foster dialogue and trust among states and enable nations to engage constructively in preventing possible flashpoints capable of disrupting global economic equilibrium. They can also check the balance of opposing interests, control possible trade conflicts, and encourage healthy competition, thus creating an environment conducive to sustained economic activities.

To summarise, developing powerful partners and alliances will enhance the future of global economic competition frameworks, making them more efficient and productive.

Amid the persistent challenges of the global economy, countries must establish productive relationships to achieve a sustainable, interdependent, and successful economy for the future.

Final thoughts: Developing Competition Strategies

Like many sectors across the globe, international relations, too, seem to change. The focus of international relations would be on the economic rivalry between countries. Combining trade and technological advancements along with collaborations generates competition strategies. Regarding economic rivalry, the future certainly appears to require a diverse approach. First and foremost, including new technologies in economic systems is of utmost importance. The quest for technological superiority must come with a degree of ethical considerations. Forwarding and inflaming relations, nations must be ready to bring forth collaborative opportunities. Further, the structure of supply chains and market dependence show how integrated the world economy is. Policymakers must analyse how the public depends on each other to set limits and avoid sabotaging themselves. These dependencies and rivalry are bound to create risks, and amidst rivalry, resiliency is paramount. Intellectual property rights and innovation dependencies are also pivotal to consider. With innovations spurring the economies, protecting property while ensuring free spaces to innovate is necessary to retain strategic economies without igniting disputes. Furthermore, the economy can also be shaped greatly by the impacts and changes a nation's currency goes through and on global financial markets.

Effective control of monetary policies and a balanced exchange rate is critical for sustaining international trade and avoiding negative repercussions. In addition, the participation of multinational companies in global conflicts profoundly reveals the merging of economy and politics. Not only do they affect market competition, but they also affect international relations and the balance of power in the world. The economic competition also evolves due to government intervention and the adoption of economic protectionism. There is a thin line between fostering economic growth and protecting local businesses, which is a burden for policymakers. These restrictions must be addressed so that a country is not isolated and trade is less one-sided. These combined factors indicate that adapting to economic conflict will require more cautious diplomacy, better planning, and coordinated discussion. Unilateral and multi-forum approaches may help resolve hostile issues and reach favourable results. Creating funded bonds and alliances beyond established political boundaries could contribute immensely to the future, aiding them in changing the notion of development. While there will always be healthy competition, we must redirect our focus to harnessing these economic conflicts as an opportunity and move towards the daunting tasks posed by the global economy.

Military Dynamics and Security Concerns

Overview of Strategic Doctrines

Understanding the evolution of strategic doctrines is crucial, as it provides a historical context and enhances our comprehension of the current state of military strategies. These doctrines, which form the basis of a state's policy on national defence, have profoundly impacted and defined the military policies and activities of nations throughout history. They include deterrent forces and conflict resolution strategies and are shaped by military technological innovations and broader geopolitical transformations. Each era, including the contemporaneous, has been characterised by the emergence of new paradigms and approaches, from the constructionist theories of deterrence in the Cold War to hybrid warfare, cyber defence, and warfare in contemporary times.

Strategic doctrines today integrate traditional and non-linear facets of security, revealing a blend of complexity and depth. States are struggling with asymmetric warfare, cyber warfare, and WMD proliferation, all of which demand a change in strategic vision and policy design. In addition, the combination of economic interdependence with geopolitical rivalry has complicated strategic thinking within policymaking, further blurring the lines of framework guiding states as they try to serve their interests while preventing dangerously volatile escalation scenarios.

The emergence of competition among major powers, particularly between older and newly industrialised countries, has driven the need to revise existing strategic doctrines.

The changes in global power infrastructure and the likelihood of some regions serving as hotspots require attention to the details of capabilities and military intentions. This could be done through a reconsideration of classical concepts of offence and defence or through acquiring relevant technological advancements. Nations are faced with the need to develop more nimble and flexible strategic doctrines to deal with their security issues.

As a result, even from the introduction of strategic doctrines, one can notice gaps in discourse and the ongoing debate on military policies at the international level, as well as the guiding frameworks on why military actions are sometimes taken. However, this will suffice to show the context within which these dynamics operate and provide a framework to appreciate the role of peace, stability, and cooperation in international relations.

Comparative Military Capabilities

When comparing nations' military capabilities, it is important to consider multiple aspects of their power, as well as the intricacies of contemporary warfare. Military capability evaluation includes all elements of war, such as manpower, technology, and equipment, alongside important logistics support, cyber capabilities, intelligence assets, and strategic force projection. Military investment, training, and doctrine shape each nation's capabilities uniquely. These elements help assess the balance of power, probable vulnerabilities, and competition spots. Maintaining these facets shows that in evaluating military capabilities, analysing the nations' defence budget, technological development, force structure, and strategic posture is imperative. Such information explains the prioritisation patterns in terms of spending and the strengths and weaknesses of the nation.

Furthermore, a comprehensive analysis of a nation should include qualitative factors, which are leadership, morale, training standards, operational readiness, and overall atmosphere. Evaluating comparison approaches in military capabilities requires considering geographical provisions or constraints, which indelibly shape a nation's power projection and national interest defence capability. Anticipating possible outcomes in the form of precise policies for defending the country supported by a deep understanding of military doctrines and strategies offers solid grounds for effective policies.

Emphasising the need for a comprehensive analysis of a nation's military potential, this approach provides a structured manner to develop effective military strategies, ensure national security, prevent hostile action, and maintain order. Explaining the changing relationships of military power requires consideration of nuclear potentials, missile defences, unmanned aerial systems, and hypersonic weapons. In light of threats being globalised, understanding military power has partnerships and strategic alliances adds intellect to the analysis. Alongside conventional forces, asymmetric threats and unconventional warfare tactics increase the scope for evaluating military power. Information warfare, cyber operations, and space capabilities redefine the criteria of military supremacy and demand comprehensive evaluation of a nation's strength. The ever-evolving nature of international relations calls for examining the military potential of nations in a structured manner to develop an appropriate set of policies for military strategies, ensure national security, prevent hostile action, and maintain order.

Nuclear Deterrence and Arms Control

Nuclear deterrence and arms control, among the earliest and most deeply held concepts in the strategic world of great power competition, are now more urgent than ever. The security policies of the system's major states have international ramifications commensurate with the escalatory nature of their nuclear doctrines. These doctrines devise strategies to contain aggression and conflict on the one hand and avoid conflict escalation on the other. For US-China relations, the nuclear arms balance alongside arms control is critical for order on the geopolitically charged interstate relations matrix. The increasing sophistication of nuclear weapons, their delivery systems, and the growing geopolitical rivalries make the need for arms control and deterrent strategies more pressing than ever.

Understanding the fundamentals of nuclear deterrence is crucial for a clear picture of the security environment. The nuclear powers that exist today are both deeply unilateral and bilateral. With extensive nuclear arsenals, China and the United States exemplify the two ends of the lever. Arms control and deterrence of the two states are essential components of the whole power calculus after analysing important political developments. To have a clear picture of the security environment, it is important to study the logic behind the nuclear set of doctrines and norms drafted by a state and the basics of its counter-deterrence strategy. In this light, exploring the concepts of first-strike ability, no-first-use policy, strategic ambiguity, and other elements of US-China relations becomes important in understanding the fundamentals of nuclear deterrence.

Exploring the historical development of arms control treaties like the Intermediate-Range Nuclear Forces Treaty and New START Treaty is crucial, as it reveals significant bilateral and multilateral efforts to curb the proliferation and potential arms racing of nuclear weapons. These efforts are a testament to the international community's commitment to maintaining peace and security. Understanding the context and implications of these treaties is essential for anyone interested in international relations and security studies.

Amid the rising tensions and military posture within the Pacific Theatre, the region's credibility and transparency in nuclear deterrence remain highly sensitive. Effective arms control regimes incorporating confidence-building, transparency, and verifiable limits to the nuclear arsenal are most important in containing strategic rivalries. Thus, seeking new avenues for future arms control negotiations and building consensus on missile defence, conventional force asymmetries, advanced weapon systems, and emerging technologies are essential for strategic stability and risk mitigation. In light of this, promoting diplomacy and expert discussion to advance international nuclear law and encourage responsible nuclear conduct becomes crucial for ensuring mutual protection against conflict escalation through miscalculation. In the end, studying the balance of nuclear deterrence and arms control within US-China relations calls for understanding the difficult realities of global security's future.

Maritime Power: The Pacific Theatre

The maritime zone has become one of the critical areas of

geo-strategic concurrences, as it has invariably been; the region of the globe in the Pacific holds great significance concerning the geo-strategics of the planet, which marks it as a hotbed of international interest. The multifunctional nature of marine power in the seaside region leaves both possibilities and obstacles to the standpoints of global superpowers. The hulls of boats, which constitute, at length, the methods of fighting, at once demonstrate the agitated character of dispute within the Pacific of the globe.

The clash of power due to economic growth and globalisation in the underdeveloped regions of the South comes hand in hand with growing debates about international conflict prudence. This part of the ocean has been ascribed the role of a battlefield where peripheral parts of the water, along with resistive caps, are incessantly fighting. A relentless struggle for dominance climbs back in order to transform the South coast into the upper sphere, requiring crashing into the fence of marketing in North Korea and Japan with border industry grenade borders.

A global makeover of the world's economy defending unique trade corresponds to grabbing energy knee backward mercantile navy...

Ensuring the safeguarding of freedom of navigation and enforcement of international maritime law remains a key area of concern for participants in the aforementioned region. Furthermore, naval forces taking on roles such as humanitarian aid and disaster relief showcase non-traditional security tasks, emphasising the diverse responsibilities of maritime powers in fostering stability and resilience.

Cross-boundary dialogues and cooperative security approaches are critical tools for managing debates on the multilateral level, building trust, creating measurement frameworks, and developing crisis response strategies. Facilitating disputes and fostering peaceful coexistence follow the contour of a rules-based order. In addition, miscalculation risks and tensions can be reduced and eased through the transparency of military actions, signing internationally recognised treaties, and adherence to norms. Focus on joint training and cooperative initiatives enhances the operational capability of naval forces and fosters understanding and trust among them.

The strategic reasoning of maritime power in the Pacific Theatre propels onward competition between currents of leading world nations. Individually scrutinising naval doctrines, port-force, and operational concepts is vital in understanding the implications of maritime activity on regional stability and global security.

Cybersecurity Threats and Defence

Cybersecurity, now the most pressing problem for governments internationally, is drawing attention due to rising internet vulnerabilities of critical infrastructure, government entities, and businesses. The structure of national security strategies is changing, as the possibility of cyber-attacks and their ramifications on essential infrastructure poses enormous risks. The study of cybersecurity threats and defence reveals that the asymmetric nature of cyber warfare possesses the destructive capability to dismantle the very systems that modern societies rely on. Active cyber espionage, cyber-attacks, theft of intellectual assets, and other non-state and state-sponsored assaults have become the new normal in cyberspace.

To effectively manage cybersecurity, each domain requires understanding various forms of threats, such as state-sponsored cyber espionage, cybercrime motivated by financial gain, and malicious disabling of vital services, which are so different from one another. It is now evident that a breach of services must be guarded against by having detection systems, encryption technologies, automated system monitoring, and organised intelligence gathering about the threats in place. Besides these measures, equipping a nation's defence forces with advanced response skills to mitigate impacts from breaches is also crucial.

The changing cyber warfare paradigm is not only in the military domain, as traditional forms of escalation and retaliation become difficult to apply. Therefore, formulating international customs and agreements to behave responsibly in cyberspace is vital for systematic cyber defence. A formalised system of collective cyber defence is formed when countries cooperate to tackle transnational cybercrime by sharing information, conducting joint exercises, or engaging in diplomatic conversations.

Additionally, the interrelation between critical infrastructures highlights the importance of collaboration between the private and public sectors in strengthening resilience against cyber-attacks. Creating and applying industry-wide standards, best practices, and regulatory policies leads to establishing a proactive cyber-defence environment. Balancing rapid technological advancements with guarded expectations allows stakeholders to address emerging cyber vulnerabilities preemptively.

The diverse components of cybersecurity require ongoing attention, flexibility, responsiveness, and strategic planning. As technological advancement and geopolitical rivalry intensify, the construction of fortified cybersecurity frameworks becomes an essential pillar in maintaining the security of societies and the global economy.

Space as the New Battleground

Space has historically been largely considered a domain of peaceful exploration and scientific activities. However, as technology advances, space is increasingly becoming a focal point of militaristic and strategic importance. Now, we examine the ongoing "space race" and the conflicts that may arise in this new territory.

Recent technological changes, along with the advent of satellite-based communication, navigation, remote sensing, and intelligence, have ushered in an era of new warfare or modern warfare. Acknowledging the importance of space capabilities to support ground-based operations, many countries are increasingly developing and safeguarding their space assets.

The growing reliance on space infrastructure by both military and civilians has led to increased worry about potential risks and the likelihood of hostile actions being executed. Anti-satellite weapons, asymmetrical threats due to cyber warfare or electronic warfare, and, to some extent, the policy of laissez-faire towards space invite the need for vigorous and effective defensive efforts.

The territorial expansion of nations raises several issues concerning leadership and jurisdiction. The lack of an overarching policy governing space activities or preventing the militarisation of space creates an already complex geopolitical situation.

At this point, discussion and cooperation on an international level become key elements. Determining behavioural norms for space, limiting the danger of accidents or collisions, and increasing transparency regarding activities conducted in orbit are fundamental for stability and avoiding escalation.

Moreover, the race for supremacy in space affects the power equilibrium and stability of the world. More than just the military aspects, the consequences involve the economy, technology, and even diplomacy. Grasping the depth of outer space as a new theatre of conflict requires an understanding of different fields combined with responsible actions to protect shared interests.

As the debate on space militarisation and defence policies becomes integral to modern security discussions, understanding the consequences for international affairs while developing relations to restrain the militarisation of space is vital.

Alliances and Strategic Partnerships

Developing global relations and military security are some areas most significantly impacted by alliances and strategic partnerships. Building strong relations increases a nation's power and capability, improving deterrence and collective security against shared dangers. We need to pay attention to the importance of alliances and strategic partnerships in intensifying great power rivalries between the US and China, alongside the impacts on the wider international relations arena.

The formation of alliances is a crucial factor in preserving the balance of international relations. The United States, for instance, has historically directed its global security strategy towards fostering meaningful alliances with like-minded countries, such as Japan, South Korea, Australia, and the NATO allies. These alliances serve as a cornerstone of U.S. foreign policy and bolster its stance against adversary contestation. Similarly, China has been forging strategic partnerships through initiatives like the Belt and Road Initiative, aiming to bolster its economic and geopolitical influence from Asia to Africa and Europe.

In this context, the sprawling cooperation network blends different interests, creating intricate diplomatic and strategic problems. The AUKUS trilateral pact and ASEAN-led multilateral security dialogues exemplify more contemporary alliances seeking to cope with emerging security challenges. Furthermore, the reciprocal defence treaties and security guarantees formulate a cohesive approach within the region to respond to crises, demonstrating the collaborative efforts to maintain peace and stability.

However, the alliance landscape also faces underlying challenges, such as the differing threat assessments and strategic priorities of the member states. Striking the right balance within these partnerships, between autonomy and interdependence, necessitates agile diplomacy and constant reevaluation of collective aims. The rise of non-state actors, combined with asymmetric threats, further underscores the need to rethink traditional alliance frameworks towards more flexible forms of coalition building that can effectively counter hybrid warfare and transnational conflict.

In the future, alliances' ability to adapt and withstand changes will be critical to dealing with the intricate security setting. Cultivating further collaboration on technological development and intelligence systems is fundamental to strengthening the workings of the alliances while countering emerging risks, including cybersecurity threats and disinformation strategies. Enhancing joint military drills alongside other collaborative efforts will improve the collective defence posture and deter provocation and coercion on the state level.

The effectiveness of alliances and other forms of strategic cooperation still depends on the equilibrium of enduring commitment, trust, shared values, and resolve about global peace and security within the environment of power politics.

Bilateral and Multilateral Security Dialogues

Contestable elements of international security tend to increase over time, and so does the importance of military modernisation and innovation. Military modernisation worldwide is a contemporary phenomenon due to strategic relevance and national defence concerns, making it imperative to adapt to shifts in technology and geopolitical factors.

Both bilateral and multilateral security dialogues serve important functions in international strategic partnership development, and they significantly influence global security perspective and outlook. These dialogues are important for working on cooperation problems in security, military, and conflict resolution. The emerging complexities of the geopolitical environment bring the need to cooperate on shared security problems and increase trust and assurance among the participating nations in bilateral and multilateral settings.

Bilateral security dialogues, as the name suggests, facilitate conversations between only two countries at a time. These dialogues help in the sharing of military intelligence, joint training exercises, and coordinated operations in countering particular regional or global threats. From these dialogues, countries try to attain an amicable understanding and intention to foster a cooperation relationship that can lead to joint security endeavours.

In contrast, multilateral security dialogues deal with

various interested parties and allow the consideration of a wider scope of security matters such as arms control and nonproliferation, counterterrorism, and crisis management. Such dialogues create the opportunity for the forming of security coalitions as well as consensus, which is vital in strengthening the unity of member states under one security policy regarding the modern interconnected reality.

To engage in successful multilayered and multilayered dialogue, there must be a form of commitment to sustainability, territorial and bodily respect, and international laws. Moreover, the advocacy of wider scope inclusion of less powerful countries is vital in achieving this as these dialogues aim to construct an all-encompassing security policy.

The importance of these discussions goes beyond immediate safety issues, as they help mitigate the chances of miscalculation and increase the chances of peaceful conflict resolution. Constructive dialogue helps nations cultivate cooperation, increase resilience to threats, and contribute to global peace and security.

Achieved bilateral and multilateral security dialogues of the relations, strengthened partnerships, and fostered coalitions of international principles needed for a rules-based order. Therefore, these dialogues are crucial for determining the direction of international relations and how nations will adapt to changing security challenges.

Evaluating the Risk of Conflict Escalation

When evaluating the possibility of conflict escalation between major powers, special attention must be paid to the geopolitical flashpoints and the possible catalysts that could result in violent escalation. Constructing this catastrophic scenario necessitates a profound examination of historical confrontations, strategic analysis of contemporary capabilities, and an understanding the systems' decision-making models of the opponent's mechanisms. The most important is an assessment of what could happen from significant oversights or misinterpretations, which tend to lead to a conflict of horrifying proportions.

One principal component that requires attention when evaluating conflict escalation is the warfare domains - land, maritime, air, space and cyber warfare. Predicting the progression of conflicts requires an appreciation of the relationship between military action and other emerging threats to national security within these domains. Also, the broadening scope of modern warfare beyond the battlefield, including the economy, politics, and society, must be addressed.

Understanding new forms of conflict alongside the traditional domains highlights the need for multi-dimensional thinking. A complete risk evaluation also includes an analysis of the allies and partners of the region in question. The existence of alliances and security agreements changes the degree to which escalation is likely and any potential chances of involvement from other combatants in the scenario presented.

Moreover, the impact of proxies and non-state actors requires a thorough understanding of their motives and capabilities, which adds complexity to the assessment.

Technology developments and innovations related to military capabilities increase the chance of conflict escalation in new ways. These developments include the proliferation of autonomous weapon systems, cyber instruments, and hypersonic missiles requiring continuous monitoring and assessment. The emerging fields of artificial intelligence and quantum computing also raise concerns regarding strategic stability, crisis communication, and conflict intervention.

Another critical aspect is analysing the diplomatic off-ramps and mechanisms of de-escalation. Knowing the channels and mechanisms for crisis communication can provide a deeper understanding of the chances to ease tensions to avoid a major escalation of conflict. This involves studying past instances of successful crisis management and applying those lessons to the current situation.

In any case, evaluating conflict escalation risks requires a defined framework of multidisciplinary input from political scientists, military strategists, historians, and regional specialists. It also requires continuous monitoring, analysis, and strategic foresight to lessen the chances of crises. While any given prediction is likely wrong, an escalation assessment will increase preparedness and mitigate drastic measures necessary to avert conflict escalation.

9

Policy Choices
Steering Away from Conflict

Policy Frameworks

The intricate landscape of international relations necessitates thoroughly exploring the underpinnings of policy frameworks designed to mitigate the risk of conflict. Developing effective policy frameworks at its core requires multifaceted considerations encompassing diplomatic engagement, strategic alliances, and economic interdependence. We can discern essential principles that inform successful conflict prevention policies by delving into historical precedents and contemporary paradigms. A critical aspect of policy formulation involves the in-depth analysis of past strategies employed by nations to steer away from conflicts. By examining historical policy approaches, we gain valuable insights into the factors contributing to de-escalating tensions and avoiding destructive confrontations. By studying diplomatic engagements, peace treaties, and crisis management mechanisms of earlier eras, we unravel the complexities of navigating geopolitical challenges through astute policymaking.

Furthermore, policy frameworks are intricately tied to fostering diplomatic engagement and dialogue mechanisms. Effective communication channels, negotiation structures, and conflict resolution protocols furnish the cornerstone of successful policy frameworks geared towards conflict prevention. Culturing mutual understanding and establishing platforms for constructive discourse play pivotal roles in averting potential hostilities and fostering enduring peace. By exploring the intricate tapestry of economic interdependence and policy strategies, we uncover the profound impact of trade relationships, economic incentives, and deterrence mechanisms in deterring conflict. Interwoven with policy frameworks, economic considerations serve as influential determinants in shaping the behaviour of nations on the global stage. Understanding the nuances of economic interdependencies is instrumental in formulating robust policies that dissuade adversarial pursuits and lean toward cooperative endeavours. Exploring multilateral approaches and international institutions further provides a comprehensive perspective on orchestrating policy frameworks for conflict prevention. The collaborative endeavours of nations within the framework of international organisations and cooperative platforms present an avenue for fostering collective security and deterring unilateral provocations. By leveraging the mechanisms and resources afforded by multilateral frameworks, nations can bolster their resilience against conflict-triggering dynamics and harmonise their efforts to achieve global stability.

Historical Policy Analysis: A Key to Understanding Conflict Avoidance

Throughout history, nations have grappled with the daunting challenge of avoiding conflicts that could lead to devastating consequences. Hence, understanding how states have successfully avoided conflict and maintained peaceful relations amidst tensions, is of utmost importance. By examining pivotal moments in international relations, we can glean invaluable insights into the nuanced diplomacy and strategic decisions that have averted potential crises. The study of historical policy analysis provides a rich tapestry of diplomatic manoeuvres, negotiated settlements, and visionary leadership that have mitigated tensions and upheld stability.

This exploration is essential for understanding the complexities of conflict avoidance and the underlying principles that inform effective policy frameworks. Examining historical policy analysis illuminates the multifaceted approaches states employ to mitigate conflicts. Case studies from various epochs shed light on the significance of proactive diplomacy, crisis management, and the cultivation of mutual interests. Historical precedent underscores the efficacy of sustained dialogue in diffusing volatile situations, whether through establishing communication channels, diplomatic missions, or peace treaties.

Moreover, the astute navigation of power dynamics, cultural sensitivities, and economic interdependencies emerge as instrumental factors in shaping policies that deter conflict. It becomes evident that historical policy analysis serves as a repository of valuable strategies, highlighting the enduring relevance of preventive diplomacy and conflict resolution mechanisms. By dissecting past instances of successful conflict avoidance, policymakers and scholars can gain crucial insights into the intricacies of international relations and the challenges inherent in maintaining global peace and stability. Ultimately, this historical perspective equips decision-makers with a nuanced understanding of the delicate balance required to avoid conflict, thereby contributing to the contemporary discourse on fostering cooperative and harmonious relationships among nations.

Diplomatic Engagement and Dialogue Mechanisms: Shaping International Relations

Diplomatic engagement and dialogue mechanisms are pivotal in shaping international relations and mitigating conflicts between nations. The art of diplomacy, characterised by tact, discretion, and negotiation, has historically been instrumental in averting crises and fostering mutual understanding. In today's interconnected world, where geopolitical tensions can escalate rapidly, the importance of diplomatic engagement cannot be overstated. It involves the active participation of diplomatic representatives and envoys in dialogue with their counterparts from other countries, allowing for the exchange of perspectives, grievances, and proposals in a structured and formalised manner. This communication platform is crucial for managing disagreements, building trust, and exploring potential avenues for cooperation. Effective dialogue mechanisms are essential for de-escalating tensions and maintaining open communication channels. Diplomats seek to identify common ground and bridge divergent interests through initiatives such as bilateral talks, multilateral negotiations, and high-level summits. Moreover, engaging in diplomatic discussions enables stakeholders to address emerging issues proactively, thus preventing misunderstandings from escalating into confrontations.

Furthermore, diplomatic engagement extends beyond crisis management and conflict resolution; it also serves as a conduit for cultural exchange and people-to-people interactions. Cultural diplomacy promotes artistic, educational, and intellectual exchanges between nations, fosters mutual respect and enhances cross-cultural understanding. This, in turn, contributes to creating resilient relationships that withstand geopolitical pressures. In contemporary geopolitics, technological advancements have revolutionised diplomatic engagement, offering new opportunities for virtual diplomacy and digital dialogue forums. Social media platforms, online conferences, and virtual diplomatic missions have become integral tools for fostering connections and dialogue, especially during physical restrictions or global crises. Effective diplomatic engagement and dialogue mechanisms ultimately require diplomats to possess astute negotiation skills, cultural sensitivity, and an acute awareness of geopolitical nuances. By establishing sustainable communication channels and embracing a spirit of collaboration, nations can navigate complex international landscapes with greater confidence and promote peaceful coexistence in an interconnected world.

Economic Interdependence and Policy Strategies: A Strategic Perspective

In the complex landscape of international relations, economic interdependence has emerged as a fundamental determinant of state behaviour and policy formulation. Nations are interconnected through intricate trade, finance, and investment networks, creating a web of economic relationships that transcend geopolitical boundaries. There is a need to understand the critical nexus between economic interdependence and policy strategies, elucidating the multifaceted dynamics that govern this symbiotic relationship. As globalisation accelerates the integration of economies, the strategic implications of economic interdependence become increasingly pronounced, shaping governments' decision-making processes worldwide. The intertwined nature of modern economies underscores the need for astute policy measures that leverage economic interdependence to foster stability and cooperation while mitigating potential risks. Strategic policymakers are tasked with navigating the delicate balance between leveraging economic interdependence as a tool for conflict prevention and managing vulnerabilities associated with overreliance on interlinked global markets. Moreover, the intricate interplay between economic and security imperatives necessitates a nuanced approach to policy formulation, wherein economic interdependence is strategically harnessed to bolster geopolitical stability and fortify diplomatic ties. At the crux of this discourse lies the exploration of diversified policy strategies to optimise the benefits of economic interdependence while safeguarding national interests. From tariff negotiations and trade agreements to investment frameworks and currency arrangements, the arsenal of policy tools available to policymakers is extensive and dynamic.

Furthermore, examining the pivotal role of economic diplomacy in constructing resilient partnerships and defusing potential sources of conflict is necessary to emphasise the role of economic interdependence as a catalyst for fostering diplomatic dialogue and mutual understanding among nations. Amidst the intricate tapestry of international economics, articulating coherent policy strategies becomes imperative in addressing the challenges and opportunities presented by economic interdependence. By charting a course that capitalises on the interconnectedness of global economies, policymakers can forge pathways toward sustainable development, collaborative prosperity, and peaceful coexistence. Concurrently, adept policy formulation is a bulwark against the destabilising effects of economic frictions, underpinning the foundational principles of global governance and multilateral cooperation. Thus, as we delve into the intricate interplay of economic interdependence and policy strategies, a comprehensive understanding of this paradigm emerges, unravelling the intricate threads that bind nations in an era defined by shared economic destinies.

Multilateral Approaches and International Institutions

The promotion of peace, stability, and cooperation on a global scale necessitates the utilisation of multilateral approaches and international institutions. These entities serve as crucial platforms for dialogue, negotiation, and the formulation of unified strategies in addressing shared challenges. Multilateralism fosters a sense of collective responsibility among nations, emphasising the significance of collaboration and consensus-building. International organisations such as the United Nations, World Trade Organization, International Monetary Fund, and various regional bodies play pivotal roles in facilitating multilateral engagement. They provide venues for deliberation, dispute resolution, and the establishment of normative frameworks governing the conduct of states in the international arena. One of the fundamental advantages of multilateral approaches is their capacity to promote inclusivity and representation.

By involving diverse stakeholders in decision-making processes, these mechanisms enhance the legitimacy and effectiveness of policies and agreements. Moreover, multilateralism allows for the pooling of resources and expertise, enabling nations to address complex issues that transcend individual capacities. Whether it pertains to climate change, global health crises, or security threats, the collaborative efforts facilitated by international institutions can yield comprehensive and sustainable solutions. Within the realm of international relations, multilateral approaches also contribute to the cultivation of trust and confidence among nations. Countries bolster mutual understanding and respect by engaging in joint initiatives and upholding shared commitments, thereby mitigating potential sources of conflict.

Furthermore, participatory involvement in multilateral forums enables states to demonstrate their willingness to adhere to common standards and principles, fostering an environment conducive to peaceful coexistence and cooperation. Nevertheless, multilateralism's effectiveness hinges upon member states' commitment to uphold the principles of equity, transparency, and accountability. The functionality of international institutions is contingent upon the willingness of nations to honour their obligations and engage in good-faith negotiations.

Additionally, the adaptability and responsiveness of these structures to evolving global dynamics are paramount in ensuring their relevance and impact. In conclusion, utilising multilateral approaches and international institutions holds immense promise in addressing the international community's multifaceted challenges. By embracing the principles of cooperation, inclusivity, and shared responsibility, nations can forge a path towards a more secure, prosperous, and harmonious world.

Domestic Policy Impacts on International Relations

A nation's domestic policy is very important in shaping its foreign relations. The balance between internal politics, economic policies, and social activities greatly defines a country's international image. This part studies the effects of domestic policies on the international stage and tries to understand the relations between international diplomacy and other geostrategic relations.

This is an important study which examines the great importance of concepts of domestic policies and their relevance to the values and priorities strategy of diplomacy. The policies governing trade and international relations, immigration, human rights, and the environment as clear examples of policies which govern the economy and aspects of the country that influence outward relations do have far-reaching impacts on the foreign policy of any nation and the diplomacy of any country. The issue of labour rights and social healthcare and education defines welfare, equity, and social justice in a country.

Furthermore, aligning domestic policies with international agreements and norms is paramount in shaping a country's relations with other states. This alignment, demonstrated through states' cooperation on climate change, human rights obligations, and general treaties, underscores the significant impact of a country's policy on international relations. Conversely, policies that deviate from these norms can lead to strained diplomatic relations, hindering efforts to foster cooperation and mutual understanding.

Moreover, the same issues consider the impact of local political relationships on the state's international relations. The reasoning of the ruling ideology, the policy-making structures, and the presence of some socio-political groups put a country's outward policies into the designed strategies. Evaluation of these policies, particularly through the lens of historical case studies, provides a comprehensive understanding of the role of domestic policies at a global level, where interactions culminate into forming alliances, treaties, and conflicts.

As we analyse domestic policies in the context of global issues, it becomes increasingly evident how a cohesive internal governance system interacts with diplomacy. Combined, these two elements provide a more nuanced approach to global encounters. This understanding and strategic foresight are crucial for addressing complex international issues and creating new avenues for international relations by collaborating with policymakers and other relevant actors.

Risk Management and Crisis Prevention Policies

Policies to manage risks and prevent crises are essential when dealing with peace and sociopolitical relations. These two strategies are very important when dealing with modern developments. There is abundant evidence showing how issues stemming from one nation can quickly spread to other regions and even countries, leading to a geopolitical crisis that can affect several nations. Therefore, it is paramount to introduce measures to prevent such things from happening. A thorough approach that analyses the region's political, economic, and socio-cultural orientation would provide an ideal preventive strategy. A more positive approach would include focusing on diplomacy and attention to lowering conflict. Nations and international organisations must collaborate to establish greater collaboration and trust in one another.

In addition, conflict mediation and peacekeeping have to be incorporated into the existing tension prevention policies for conflict prevention. Sustaining and establishing the interaction lines towards the conflicting parties is fundamental for tranquil conflict resolution and de-escalation. In addition, creating confidence-building measures and frameworks for crisis communication can lessen the chances of profound tension, misunderstanding, or miscalculation during high-tension periods. Moreover, active intervention policies concerning peace strategy have to increase the restraint of taking unilateral actions concerning openness and accountability in international relations. Unobstructed communication and transparency are important in the actions which aid in averting conflict and reducing the possibility of conflict escalation.

Risk and crisis prevention is achieved in international relations by assessing the changing geopolitical landscape. As is clear, unanticipated risks and challenges require new approaches. One such approach is the 'Adapt and Evolve' policy strategy, which involves continuously adapting and evolving policies to address emerging risks and challenges. Furthermore, crisis prevention policies can be much more effective when they are internationally coordinated due to the synergy gained towards minimising conflicts. The synergy enables collaboration in intelligence gathering, scenario planning, resource deployment, and addressing potential threats. Diplomacy, negotiation, and other benign resolution strategies should provide the framework for all conflict prevention policies. Nations can avert possible escalations and sustainable international and national stability while focusing on dialogue and disregarding diplomacy.

Role of Leadership in Shaping Foreign Policy

The organisational structure should change to divide the roles as follows:

Global Affairs – Adopt an approach that allows leadership to define nurtured policies.

Foreign Affairs—Enable unitary accounts of specialists' engagement in the country's forward relations. 'Forward relations refer to proactive engagement with other countries and international organisations to shape the country's future international standing and influence. This involves strategic planning, negotiation, and the establishment of alliances and partnerships.

Global leaders and sides of policy should derive their policies from the actions of specific leaders who head the country that actively engages in war, which also happens to be a superpower looming over the shoulders of every other nation. Clear leadership strategies shape each nation in global operations, making leadership a critical aspect driving foreign policies.

Making decisions in foreign policy requires careful thought not just of the choices, but also of the web of diplomatic, economic, and security factors that come into play. As a leader moves through trade deals, multilateral dealings, and security matters, there is a heavy burden to consider the state of their country in the international system. The policies that are crafted should attend to both the country's long-term goals while taking immediate concerns into account.

Building and fostering relationships with other world actors is one of the defining traits of leadership in foreign policy. Leaders can build trust, offer dialogue, and foster cooperation through diplomacy and bilateral relationships. This requires negotiation, cultural intelligence, and a deep knowledge of the history one is dealing with in international relations.

Leadership in foreign policy is about principled and ethical conduct toward the world. Leaders must respect the boundaries and values set by their countries in terms of inclusivity, human rights, and international law. The conduct of any foreign actors is critical as it shapes the image of the country and the expectations of other countries in the world.

Leaders are also responsible for effective crisis management and conflict resolution. The way nations deal with international crises, militarily or diplomatically, often shapes a country's foreign policy and image within the international community. Strong leadership requires flexibility, the capacity to remain calm under pressure, and the disposition to peacefully resolve controversial matters.

To conclude, the leadership role in formulating foreign policy is complex, burdensome, and multidimensional. It needs foresight, thoughtful assessment, and amalgamation of the state's needs and the international community's objectives. In the context of the world's change, leaders are central in dealing with the complexities of international relations in a manner that fosters peace, security, and development for the state and even for the world community.

Case Studies: Successful De-escalation Efforts

Studying international relations offers significant value when examined through a de-escalation effort lens; international relations gives away social, political, and military dimensions. Successfully blending these competing perspectives and forging peace out of conflict showcases absolute diplomatic and strategic competence. One prominent example of successful de-escalation is the 1962 Cuban Missile Crisis. US President John F. Kennedy and Soviet Premier Nikita Khrushchev, each governing superpowers during a heightened period of arms conflict, put their nations' heads to a gruelling standoff, interspersed with intense negotiations and so-called give-and-take to avoid a nuclear war. Confrontation between both forces was avoided by refraining from accepting surrender and de-escalation of martyrdom.

In 1978, another compelling example came in the form of the Camp David Accords, persistently negotiated and finalised under the supervision of US President Jimmy Carter. Egyptian President Anwar Sadat and Israeli counterpart Menachem Begin brokered a peace treaty after years of deep-rooted conflict. The accords remain an unprecedented achievement of sustained diplomacy as they inspire not just former conflicting states but negotiators all over the globe.

In a more recent context, the Iran Nuclear Deal, or Joint Comprehensive Plan of Action (JCPOA), reduced the escalating tensions between Iran and the global powers. Negotiations were made to reach common ground through painstaking diplomacy, inviting Iran to curb its nuclear ambitions instead of relaxed sanctions. This demonstrated effective multilateralism's prospects in addressing intricate geopolitical problems.

Also worth noting is the 1989 Taif Agreement, which was pivotal in ending the Lebanese civil war. The agreement emphasised the role of dialogue and inclusive mediation in some of the deep-rooted disputes. This provided an overarching framework for national reconciliation and power sharing, which was made possible by continuous diplomacy towards age-old rivalry.

The cases discussed show how actively and ethically driven diplomacy of sustained engagement can resolve crises and facilitate conflicts. Exploring the details of the strategies and defining moments of these processes of successful de-escalation reveals the sheer complexity of conflict resolution and the strategies that lie beneath sustainable peacebuilding.

Conclusion: Strategic Decisions for Continued Future Peace

Strategic choices are essential for future stability, as seen in the analysis of successful conflict de-escalation examples. The combination of historical case studies and contemporary diplomacy highlights the importance of conflict management through careful decision-making. International actors must ensure that sustainable peace and collaboration are achieved through strategic policies in the future.

Future stability strategic decisions should include lessons from history and the intricacies of interstate relations. Policymakers should advocate for a sustained approach by effectively applying diplomacy, economic cooperation, and multilateralism. Moreover, international affairs' intricate relationships require pragmatic policies to be formulated considering the domestic aspects of international relations.

While developing strategic options, risk management and crisis avoidance policies are vital for minimising possible conflicts. Averted violence is usually handled with dialogue and conflict resolution protocols that mitigate rising tensions and encourage peaceful coexistence. This information indicates that the role of leadership is crucial in the formulation of foreign affairs since visionary leaders lead nations in responsible and active engagement.

Informed decisions about the future of a country have to be made with attention to the complex modern international relations systems that require an understanding of the interrelations of power and contemporary difficulties. For that reason, the approaches intended to maintain stability in the future are those with flexibility and rigorous planning, as policies need to change reliably to address the challenges emerging in the global sphere. Balanced policy through systematised self-reflection assists in analysing what does and what does not work to maintain geopolitical equilibrium.

To sum up, the strategic options for future sustainability aim to actively prevent future conflicts and nurture peace within the global community. Through historical and contemporary practices, policymakers can navigate towards enduring peace and constructive relations. Countries and their leaders must embrace strategic foresight to work towards a greater good for all and make informed decisions for a stable and prosperous world.

10

Global Challenges
Opportunities for US-China Cooperation

The Necessity of Collaborative Global Governance

Collaborative global governance is crucial in an increasingly interconnected and interdependent world. The US and China are the world's two greatest powers and, therefore, need to manage international relations and collective action regarding global public goods. This chapter will discuss how both countries can amend and change their global governance policies.

For effective global governance, cooperation and coordinated action across all countries are needed to address issues that cut across national borders. The international cooperation model, which has been usual for a long time in which states are solo actors exercising their sovereign rights, is no longer tenable, with sophisticated problems like climate change, pandemics, cybersecurity, and inequality becoming common. This makes it essential for the US and China to have dialogues and take steps towards changing their ideas about global governance systems.

One factor that requires attention is the alteration of international systems and the creation of new ones that capture evolving global politics. Both countries may use their diplomatic relations and soft power to give attention to fair and equal representation in the United Nations, the World Trade Organization, and the International Monetary Fund. Promote multilateralism and ensure that developing nations are heard and that the US and China can enhance the legitimacy and efficacy of global governance systems.

Fostering collaboration on regulatory standards and best-known practices contributes to accountability, transparency, and responsibility for trade, investment, and technology. Aligning policies and regulations reduces conflict and increases predictability within the economy, which enhances the chances of economic development within the region.

Additionally, bridging the gap and reaching a middle ground on critical issues such as climate change and humanitarian assistance is vital in facilitating the much-needed cooperation and trust between the US and China. Coordinated efforts, expertise, and resources towards humanitarian and disaster relief showcase commitment to the values and responsibilities within the international sphere.

As major world players, the US and China have the

responsibility to set a precedent in supporting reforms for global governance systems and structures. With better communication, respect, and compromise from both sides, both powers can help achieve a more stable order internationally.

Addressing Climate Change: A Shared Responsibility

It is evident that the modernisation of society presents numerous issues, one of them being climate change, which requires urgent action from every corner of the globe. Climate change is at stake, and it doesn't respect territorial boundaries. It is the responsibility of every nation, including the US and China. It is essential to forge strong collaboration to control climate change as both countries are the top greenhouse gas emitters. Combatting climate change requires a united front to cut emissions, increase renewable sources, and adjust to the new climate reality.

China and the US' constructive collaboration can trigger action on global climate issues. The countries can set clear renewable energy policies, scale up emission caps, and use both nations' engineering prowess as a joint scheme to pioneer a global leading example. Moreover, they will be able to advance new frontiers of innovative clean energies and sustainable practices with joint research and knowledge exchange endeavours, offering a beacon of hope in the fight against climate change.

Furthermore, the importance of environmental justice and equity gives additional context in the case of climate change solutions. The two nations have to understand the adverse effects of climate change deeply on weaker sections of society and ensure that the focus of their combined effort is at least mostly on resilience and adaptation in those areas. Also, assisting developing countries in achieving sustainable development and climate-positive changes should be a major focus of their collaboration.

Striking a balance between the climate change challenge and the need for international cooperation and partnership remains critical. The United States and China can use the available international frameworks and forums to interact with other countries, joining discussions or negotiating dealings that seek to reduce the effects of climate change. Such cooperation will strengthen openness, trust, and responsibility while enhancing respect towards each other for the world's sustainability.

In any regard, conquering the challenges of climate change comes with a responsibility to be painstaking and see the bigger picture from the outset. Addressing problems related to the economy and society's social issues requires well-defined frameworks. At this defining moment for the US and China, these two leading nations focusing on dealing with climate change as a primary need demonstrate exemplary leadership and responsibility in nurturing the world that future generations will inhabit.

Public Health and Pandemics: Strengthening Joint Preparedness

In an era where globalisation is at full throttle, public health alongside pandemics has become one of the most paramount issues that require utmost attention towards readiness and prevention at the global level. This was best seen during the COVID-19 period, which truly catalysed the need for introspection into how health systems work internationally during times of outbreak. Strengthening collaborative preparedness efforts between the US and China is essential to sustain dire threats. Joint interventions should incorporate the sharing of information, early identification systems, response systems, and research for vaccines and medicine. Bolstering preemptive action requires cooperation towards transparency in reporting infectious disease data. Both countries must improve their frameworks, such as surveillance systems, resilient healthcare systems, and support for vulnerable groups.

Additionally, developing an all-encompassing plan for prompt distribution of medical supplies during sanitary crises should be incorporated. Unified lines of agreement and standards, as well as contingent universalism of experts, are necessary. Also of equal importance, a pact fortifies direct international health organisations like the WHO by inciting joint funds with reform focused on global health preparedness. This transparency in reporting infectious disease data is crucial in reassuring the public and maintaining trust in the system.

The US and China should devise quad capacity-enhancing programmes to equip healthcare workers, first responders, and other relevant professionals with the skills and knowledge necessary to handle public health emergencies competently. The need for communication, including dialogue and joint exercises, also at the highest levels on a scheduled basis is essential in improving the preparedness and responsiveness of the two nations. Furthermore, collaboration in scientific research and innovation can help develop new technologies for monitoring, diagnosing, and treating diseases. Enhanced bilateral and multilateral collaboration on public health and pandemic issues allows these two countries to work together towards achieving global health security and stability. Both nations can minimise the effects of emerging pandemics and enhance the health of the global populace through unified efforts.

Cybersecurity Threats: Establishing Common Protocols

We can all agree that cybersecurity threats are of greater concern for America and China. The threats posed to state-sponsored systems and lone hackers have an increasingly available network to leverage to inflict maximum damage. Establishing common approaches to deal with the problem has proven effective over the years. Collaborating on integrating protocols for managing systems helps limit the risk posed by attempts at cyber intrusion or cybernetic warfare.

Common approaches require the formation of direct lines of communication between relevant bodies of the two states, including their decision-making organs, as one of the primary approaches. This not only facilitates the provision of information regarding emerging threats but also aids in the joint assessment of risks and merging intelligence systems for easier accessibility. Such initiatives will greatly enhance synergy at the level of tightening the identification and mitigation of cyberinfrastructure weaknesses, boosting the robustness of responsive measures.

Furthermore, it is necessary to create common approaches for effectively dealing with advanced persistent cyber threats. This requires integrating policies and regulations regarding data privacy, incident management, and attribution of responsibility for cyber attacks. By harmonising these elements, the two countries could resolve much of the uncertainty associated with cyber incidents, which could lead to serious tensions within cyberspace.

Another important aspect of the common frameworks is the development of strong systems for mutual support for cooperative cyber defence. This includes developing bilateral emergency response plans and participating in joint cybersecurity exercises to improve incident response. Moreover, the US and China could strengthen their collective defence through joint professional education programmes for cybersecurity specialists.

Apart from cooperation at the bilateral level, it is

equally important to broaden the scope of collaboration to the international level by calling for the development of global cybersecurity policies and frameworks. Both countries need to actively participate in multilateral initiatives that encourage acceptable practices in cyberspace, build international agreements on cyber control, and actively work to prevent harmful cyber activities through international diplomatic efforts.

To conclude, it is clear that more common protocols in cybersecurity need to be established because of the unified understanding of the threat that cyber malfeasance incurs. The US and China are in a strong position to cooperate in dealing with the multi-pronged problems of cyber threats and, therefore, construct a safer cyberspace that promotes sustainable socio-economic development and global stability.

Trade Partnerships: Enhancing Economic Interdependence

The trade partnerships between China and the United States enhance economic interdependence and encourage mutual benefits. Both countries are economically powerful, and their trade relations can impact the economy on a global scale. The two countries can improve their trade relations to utilise their comparative advantages to balance their economies and achieve sustainable development. Strengthening trade partnerships also highlights the necessity to observe and promote fair trade and open market policies, which is equally beneficial for other nations.

Also, the growth of commercial relations enables the exchange of goods, services, and even capital, which sets the stage for greater integration of the global economy. The United States and China, the world's first and second largest economies, respectively, can enhance global innovation, employment, and economic growth due to their combined trade endeavours. Strategic trade cooperation provides a foundation for sustainable economic growth and strengthens bilateral relations, as it allows contentious issues to be resolved through negotiation and dialogue.

Additionally, adopting trade cooperation benefits both countries because it allows for the diversification of supply chains, which helps mitigate the impact of possible shocks, strengthening overall economic resilience. Active trade relations encourage increased access to local and international markets, boosting investment and declining regulation, thus improving resource allocation and economic productivity. Such measures help companies and customers and highlight the commitment to maintaining an open and clear international trade framework.

Fostering trade relationships also involves appreciating the relationship between trade, technology, and intellectual property law. Considering that the US and China are both major players in technological advancement, a collaborative trade policy creates a platform for dealing with issues of intellectual property rights, technology transfer, and national security related to cyberspace technology. With defined borders of cooperation in these areas, both countries will be able to take advantage of new technologies without losing control over sensitive information and ensure responsible business practices.

Strengthening the interdependence of the US and China through trade relations will lead to a more unified global economy. Collaboration in these areas is expected to result in economic growth, stimulate innovation, and create a foundation for sustainable shared wealth. Therefore, trade relations should be prioritised and developed as important measures to improve international relations and the economy for global stability and prosperity.

Scientific Research and Innovation Collaboration

The advancement of science and technology through research cooperation between the world's leading nations, the United States and China is highly beneficial, allowing the countries to solve global problems together and develop in various areas. Through scientific understanding and available resources, cooperative efforts can achieve their goals. This collaboration encompasses a broad range of fields; it includes but is not limited to, biomedical research, sustainability efforts towards the environment, space research, Artificial Intelligence, and renewable forms of energy. From the biomedical research perspective, collaborative projects can facilitate faster development in infectious disease management, cancer care, and vaccine preparations. Sharing data, resources, and relevant knowledge can easily enable researchers from both countries to make significant advancements in the healthcare industry. Additionally, collaboration in sustainability efforts towards the environment can lead to progress in addressing climate change, preserving biodiversity, and further developing and improving sustainable development. Specific steps that are advantageous to the two nations and the entire world can be developed and utilised.

The collaboration of nations is even more evident when considering space exploration as a frontier where synergy can be achieved by leveraging technological capabilities to launch into space together. Space collaboration has the potential to deepen the scientific knowledge of both nations and, in turn, enhance humanity's understanding of the possibilities related to space. Moreover, collaborative efforts towards artificial intelligence and machine learning can profoundly impact other industries, including health, transport, finance, and manufacturing. Harnessing strengths in these modern technologies can propel global advancement and development.

Significant collaborations in the field of renewable energy can be achieved through joint research projects and partnerships aimed at clean and sustainable energy sources. These efforts to advance the capture and utilisation of solar, wind, and other renewable resources not only contribute towards energy security but also play a crucial role in combating climate change. The United States and China, by synergising their expertise and resources, can accelerate the world's transition towards sustainable, low-carbon emission energy, triggering positive shifts in the global energy market.

In conclusion, collaboration through scientific research and development presents a beneficial opportunity for the United States and China to integrate their intellect and technology. The outcomes achieved when these two powerful nations collaborate can alleviate many challenges today while ensuring a better future for future generations.

Cultural Exchange: Building Mutual Understanding

Cultural exchange plays a pivotal role in fostering mutual understanding between countries, particularly given the historically delicate relationship between the US and China. Enhanced cultural exchange can help address decades-old misconceptions, improve people-to-people relations, and increase multicultural appreciation in both countries. These exchanges, which impact ordinary citizens, are more profound than diplomatic gestures and build foundations for improved bilateral relations. This is why we analyse cross-cultural relations, specifically focusing on China and the USA.

As in any cross-cultural interaction, differences in backgrounds bring with them a set of advantages and challenges. The first of these challenges is sharing ideas, traditions, and values, which necessitates the development of mutual trust and respect. International cooperation through education, language immersion, performing arts and music festivals, and academic symposiums are some initiatives that help individuals from both nations understand and appreciate each other's customs, beliefs, and social behaviours. Through these interactions, people learn to appreciate and tolerate differing ways of thinking and develop a sense of belonging to one world irrespective of borders.

In addition, cultural exchanges facilitate an unprecedented opportunity for people to appreciate and celebrate each other's heritages while highlighting differences that are more significant than nationality.

Also, cultural exchange is an important means of breaking stereotypes and misconceptions. For both the US and China, personal exchanges allow both nations to put a human face to the other and loosen the prejudices and biases each side has of them. Participants can build genuine relationships by bringing people together through artists' residencies, youth leadership programmes, and other cooperative culture showcases, thereby changing perceptions and dismantling deep-seated barriers that prevent proper understanding. Through these relationships, history is re-written, creating a network of trust and friendship that crosses the borders of diplomacy and politics. In this way, soft power becomes an invaluable aid to expansion through cultural interaction diplomacy, fostering an open atmosphere for positive and constructive discussion and collaboration.

Cultural exchange not only widens the scope of understanding different cultures, but also drives other areas like economic development and tourism. The merging of cultural identity through joint projects like heritage conservation or culinary crossovers, and even culture-induced tourism, brings further growth and development. This potential for mutual growth and development through cultural exchange is a reason for optimism and hope.

When people take a real interest in each other's culture, it not only increases the demand for cultural goods, artistic works, and tourism, but also creates an economic advantage for both nations' creative industries and local economies. This self-sustaining system fosters growth and investment in emerging cultures and innovations as well as cultural preservation, leading to a robust cultural economy. In addition, as tourists travel to visit each other's countries, they not only add to the cultural wealth of the visited country, but also take back positive testimonials that encourage other people to visit and become goodwill advocates, multiplying the prospects for cultural exchange.

In essence, the possibilities posed by cultural exchange in the US and China relationship are limitless. By appreciating and valuing each other's cultures and heritage, both countries stand to gain a better understanding of the intricate details of the international community. This understanding is what builds strong and lasting partnerships regardless of shifts in politics or geopolitical contexts. The limitless possibilities of cultural exchange should inspire and motivate the audience to prioritise and invest in it.

Navigating Geopolitical Tensions in the Asia-Pacific

Due to its complexity, dynamism, and depth, there is a need for advanced engagement strategies and meticulous diplomacy in dealing with the geopolitical tensions of the Asia-Pacific region. Given the Asia Pacific's history as an international economic engine and a strategic focal point, it is vital to understand its culture and politics in detail. This region suffers from uncertainty due to persistent violent sentiment due to historical grudges, military aggressiveness, and territorial squabbles. These factors require more than one solution – they need attention to history and contemporary geopolitical realities. A dialogue conducive to conflict resolution and de-escalation of prior animosities must be established. Moving forward, finding solutions requires taking into consideration the multiple viewpoints of the different nations in the region. As the primary players in the Asia Pacific, China and the United States have shaped the region's geopolitics, and so have the other nations. The implications of their cooperative or confrontational interactions are much stronger than their visible sphere of influence. Considering their interdependence, managing geopolitical conflicts in the Asia Pacific region significantly contributes to global international relations, peace, and stability.

A comprehensive approach to managing these tensions is directly interacting with regional stakeholders through diplomatic channels, utilising international organisations to construct or encourage dialogue. In addition, confidence-building initiatives and transparency in military activities can lessen the chance of unintended escalation. Trust among nations can be built through shared activities such as joint military training exercises, humanitarian response exercises, and cultural exchanges, which foster mutual understanding and diminish suspicion. Additionally, the establishment of mechanisms for the enforcement of international law and the resolution of disputes is essential for nurturing a rule-based framework in the area. The Asia-Pacific region should henceforth be envisioned as a geopolitically stable region where peaceful coexistence, economic development, and mutual respect are core values. Stakeholders may promote a more stable and peaceful region through dialogue, cooperation, and diplomacy.

Diplomatic Engagement at Multilateral Forums

As one of the primary means of US-China relations, diplomatic engagement at forums such as the G-20 and ASEAN serves as an arena for both countries to interact positively, even with the ever-changing geopolitical relations at hand. The United Nations, G-20, and ASEAN, as obligated international cooperations, additionally provide a medium for deliberation, negotiations, and agreements towards finding solutions to different global problems. Because most, if not all, international issues such as climate change and even pandemics are globally interconnected, diplomacy in collaboration is a very crucial component.

At these multilateral forums, the US and China have great opportunities to interact at high levels with various nations and regional blocs, which encourages the free flow of ideas. Each country, by taking part in discussion and formal decision-making, assumes the position of responsibility that comes with the expectation of global citizenship and international leadership. This aids the construction of trust and good understanding and the development of accepted rules and culture for enduring peace and development.

Advance engagement at multilateral forums entails actively seeking to resolve and build conflicts. It encompasses interest-based negotiation and seeking consensus amidst differing positions. Through fundamental and clear diplomacy, the US and China can work towards aligning their goals and policies with global governance systems, thereby reducing clashes and enabling effective cooperation.

Furthermore, bilateral and multilateral forums enable stakeholders to discuss more intricate security issues, including China's maritime conflict with Japan and general issues of Asia-Pacific region stability. Both countries can use layered dialogues as well as confidence and trust-building measures to identify de-escalation, risk reduction frameworks, and rule-based conflict resolution mechanisms. Through the application of their diplomatic might and skill, the US and China can greatly impact the peace and stability of this region, whose influence on the rest of the world's order is strategically significant.

In closing, the US and China have the potential to improve trustworthy relations and collaboration between them through active engagement at multilateral forums, which in turn is constructive towards shaping enduring productive partnerships and cooperative governance on a global scale. Such leadership to solve shared concerns will constructively evaluate and foster essential change through principled policy initiatives, compromise, and promote cooperation while demonstrating strategic vision and setting a positive precedent for all.

Defining a Robust Framework for Future Cooperation

To enhance the frame of relations towards their supported projection, multilateral initiatives consisting of cooperation on joint interests and multidisciplinary diplomacy should be centralised in multilateral forums to resolve principal issues and mitigate divided interventions caused by China and the US that disharmonise the global community. Without active engagement, these forums will fail to address the gap of the underlying principal issues, such as their competition and lack of trust-building foundation initiatives sandboxed by needlessly divisive interventionism and multi-strategy dealing.

Adequate crisis management and conflict resolution procedures need to be predefined for effective strategies for future collaboration. Establishing policies to avert violence and resolve disputes will be vital to avoiding escalating conflicts into harmful geopolitical confrontations. Additionally, establishing communication systems across different levels of governance will assist in easy coordination during disputes or disagreements, ensuring little to no miscalculations.

As previously discussed, promoting reciprocal interactions and joint activities in the economic, scientific, and cultural sectors will be subnetworks for fostering other framework aspects. These joint investment ventures and technological platforms would aid in mitigating world problems while also advancing the progress of both nations by allowing them to use each other's strengths. Encouraging these academic and cultural collaborations strengthens the understanding of societal values, traditions, and aspirations, thus encouraging the social fabric that binds enduring partnerships.

The structure and strategy of cooperation should emphasise the importance of respecting international conventions and their enforcement mechanisms. The United States and China can fulfil their obligations as responsible international leaders by abiding by defined frameworks and rules within global systems. Accepting an order-based policy on international affairs will foster an ecosystem of healthy rivalry where legal disputes are resolved in reputable courts of law established by treaties and binding documents to provide justice and fairness to all parties involved.

Similarly, the vision for the cooperative structure must emphasise protecting the environment by advancing and adopting green technology, transitioning renewable energy sources, and fighting ecological warfare. Working together to mitigate climate change, protect biodiversity, and promote environmental awareness will serve the two countries and enhance global citizenship.

In other words, crafting a comprehensive structure for ongoing collaboration requires sustained effort, unwavering dedication, and a willingness to set aside differences in more universal shared objectives. Through such a lens, the US and China should be able to strategise constructive interaction aimed at stimulating bilateral relations and transforming global relations if they shift focus to moving past the historical tensions.

11

Future Scenarios
Navigating the Path Ahead

Innovation Scenarios for the Future

Puzzles and enigmas require careful reasoning and exploration; nothing fits better than understanding future scenarios. Potential scenarios are critical to strategy, planning, and policymaking from the geopolitical dimension. In exploring tomorrow's uncharted lands, it is clear that power dynamics are subject to change due to numerous factors, such as technology, changing alliances, and global partnerships. The shifting landscapes require multiple levels of adaptability and proactive anticipation, enabling one to navigate any unsettlement.

The vast scope of scenarios encourages collaboration, shared prospects, and anticipatory competition. Each proposed strategy presents growing challenges; however, it promises to offer high-requirement preemption and critical stimuli. Embracing the need to deal with change reinforces the need to act quickly in responding to change. Nations that adopt reactive policy systems to challenges are subject to ungovernable forces, which have the potential to redefine the world to an unpredictable order.

There is a direct relationship between the trends affecting our world and the need for future scenario planning that accounts for non-geopolitical factors because of the nature of our interrelated world. These scenarios demand the inclusion of economic interdependence, environmental sustainability, and technological advancement. To do so involves anticipating the many possible paths to the future that we may have to confront and be prepared for complex scenarios through strategically analysing and addressing each avenue developed through systematic observation and study. When all of these factors are considered, it tends to foster more accurate predictions regarding possible outcomes.

In general, anticipating the future and carefully monitoring and analysing world events prepare us to proactively adjust and respond before it becomes too late, prompting proactive change. When planning for the future, a clear understanding of the different scenarios and available strategies dedicated to achieving specific goals is required. Such an approach encourages leaders and policymakers to analyse future possibilities and balance risk versus opportunities to mitigate undesirable circumstances while shaping strategy for societal progress. This helps bolster stability during pressing needs and aims towards sustainable, forward-thinking development.

This exploration of future scenarios aims to sharpen our vision of international relations and world affairs. It requires focusing on current developments, potential outcomes, and balanced strategies for tackling the unexpected. The need for careful planning, flexibility, and dependable strategy for the evolving context becomes increasingly apparent in such exploration.

Analysing Current Power Dynamics

A thorough and detailed assessment encompassing all relevant aspects needs to be conducted to deconstruct the complex web of global power relations. For this purpose, it is critical to understand the geopolitical, economic, and military aspects that formulate the distribution and utilisation of power among states. From a geopolitical perspective, competition among certain world regions known as powers has enabled a distinct modification of the traditional international order. This has led to the formation of new alliances that are replacing the older ones. The Eurasian continent has become an arena of strategic competition for countries trying to gain regional power and leadership. The economic changes are also significant, as we can see with the emerging economies, which are weakening and even changing established economic paradigms. Moreover, the most recent developments in technological innovation, such as artificial intelligence, cyber warfare, and space exploration, have established a new powerful frontier which impacts the political arena. The military domain is not untouched by these developments, as the latest sophisticated weaponry and advanced asymmetric warfare methods have introduced more complexity into the equation. Studying the relationship among all these spheres is essential to understanding the basics of current power relations. It discloses a blend of elements that shape the modern world, highlighting the need to manage the complex structure of global power relations deftly. This balance of power analysis is essential for developing coherent policies to enhance international collaboration and peace while reducing tension points of competition and conflict.

Predictive Models and Their Implications

Exploring the scope of predictive models in international relations is critical, utilising their ability to uncover insight into future geopolitical events. Predictive models must be constructed based on social evolution and economic and military technologies to understand geopolitical relations. Data analytics offer foresight into scenarios and their impacts on international relations, constructing models meticulously while using historical data, real-world events, and numerous hypotheses for simulations. Analysts work day and night to develop models that aid global policies and economics. As global forecasting models gain momentum, predictors set on a journey to identify key shifting threshold markers to develop heuristics that would either guide countries from prospective conflict or allow them to dodge planned turbulence ahead. These models change the paradigm of strategy and dilemma domain theory. Even though exploitative situations and opportunities can be skillfully devised, the tip or shoulder still poses limitations with unpredictable factors altering known paths.

The consequences of these and those of such policy models require re-evaluating policies and international relations. They call for recalibration and suggest that the policies may need to be shifted to more responsive ones. Let's analyse these forecasting models a little deeper. It is clear that they not only shape our perception of the future but also compel us to evolve and rethink the models of power, with the understanding that ready, adaptable, and flexible plans are needed. With the speed of change and integration, forecasting is not limited to a region but spans continents, impacting partnerships, business, and the international governance system. Hence, these models should be studied in greater detail to understand better the paths that can be taken toward sustainable peace and development.

Potential Economic Pathways

Potential economic pathways remain important when contemplating the future of international relations. To understand interdependencies and shifting power relations, various economic pathways that could culminate in certain geopolitics must be considered. Understanding potential economic pathways provides a perspective on international relations and security amid complexity. Coupled with the rise of emerging economies, shifting trade partnership dynamics make it important to explore multiple economic scenarios to project the global order's probable future paradigm.

Based on the context, adopting a multi-disciplinary approach from engineering and social sciences, one of the steps in developing scenarios consists of exploring technological innovations and understanding how they trickle down to productivity, employment, restructuring industries, and other salient factors. Likewise, understanding the implications of various models of economic growth, such as state capitalism versus free-market capitalism, is equally important in constructing plausible future scenarios. The interface where economic force and commanding strategic resources meet warrants equal attention, especially concerning transitions in energy, achieving sustainable development goals, and competition for resources.

In seeking possible economic pathways, focus on the intricacy of economies and other global institutions which assist in smoothing economic fluctuations and bolstering stability. Also, the effects of the changing population groups and their impact on consumption, investment, and labour dynamics must be considered. Assessing the effects of regional trading blocs, investment distribution, and monetary relationships is essential towards developing a more coherent explanation of the future economy.

Most importantly, the highlighted possible economic pathways in the previous sections are valuable tools for identifying fractures or convergence points in international relations. These global economic pathways can easily be navigated under exemplary political leadership, robust strategies, or deft adjustments of relations to target potential cooperation, sources of competition, or areas requiring intervention before becoming flashpoints.

Since those areas are interconnected, exploring possible economic pathways requires advanced study of economics, geopolitics, and strategic studies. This research attempts to provide policymakers, researchers, and practitioners with distinct economic pathways, enabling them to understand global affairs' complex dynamics.

Security Strategies for Sustainable Peace

The effectiveness of security strategies dramatically contributes to the global balance of power and ensures sustainable peace. They should be based on an integrated framework that includes military, diplomatic, economic, and even technological approaches. Encouraging cooperative security frameworks between nations must come first to prevent conflict escalation and promote trust. These measures could be comprised of confidence-building exercises, greater transparency for policies dealing with defence, and more efficient crisis management systems aimed at lessening the chances of miscalculations and misunderstandings. First, conflict prevention must become a priority through early warning systems, mediation, and building the capacity to sustain in dormant regions. Sustainable peace can be achieved when the rest of the world takes responsibility for conflicts through conflict stability and psychologically unstable areas.

Furthermore, active response is critical through peacekeeping missions and humanitarian aid to address unresolved crises and protect those at risk. Aside from abusing international laws, these measures promote the maintenance of human rights vital for real order and stability in the world. At the same time, advancements in the fields of arms reduction and non-proliferation help significantly combat the dangerous issues of armed confrontations and curb access to weapons of mass destruction.

Global security challenges can be mitigated using an international approach through conventions and multi-disciplinary arms control treaties. In addition, adopting methods for technology-enabled cybersecurity and intelligence is critical in anticipation of threats in the cyber realm. Establishing responsible cyber behaviour and developing advanced cybersecurity systems and mechanisms for information exchange is the foundation of security approaches for today's world. Understanding the relationship between security and socio-economic development is equally important in addressing sustainable peace. Solving the underlying problems of people's grievances and promoting socio-economic development and social integration goes a long way in creating a peaceful environment devoid of violence, conflict and terrorism. Finally, examining the processes of successful conflict resolution and peace-building offers essential insights for structuring comprehensive regional security strategies for different contexts. The input of community members and conflict resolution experts will significantly enhance the strategies' effectiveness. With these strategies, states and the world will move toward a future of lasting peace and economic growth.

Technological Advancements as a Catalyst for Change

Substantial technological progress has been made in almost every sector of life in recent years; from the emergence of artificial intelligence to quantum computing and biotechnology, all have technologically shattered industries. With these changes, international relations and geopolitical power structures undergo profound shifts.

A nation's effort to maintain or gain new competitive advantages involves an increased focus on technological developments and technology in general. We are consequently entering a period of digital infrastructure and scientific innovation.

In the field of defence and security, technology has transformed warfare to include cyber capabilities and autonomous weaponry systems occupying crucial positions in a nation's arsenal. Additionally, the expansion race of space legions and its increasing militarisation permit a fresh perception of the entire strategy and operational lenses, further multiplying the profound importance of military high technology.

Additionally, the economic impact of technological advancements is equally essential. Disruptive innovations have revolutionised entire markets, supply chains, and workforces, both positively and negatively. The development of commerce portals, financial technology, and digital currencies has changed the world of finance, and the same is valid for work and employment with automation and artificial intelligence. On a global front, nations at the forefront of innovating new technologies tend to dominate, thereby controlling the economic power and hegemony of the world.

From a policy perspective, technology as a new phenomenon has made international cooperation more intricate and competition more fierce. Data control, cybersecurity, and safeguarding proprietary information have become significant issues for global discussion. In addition, information technologies and others that evolve rapidly create ethical and legal disputes that require mutual consideration and consensus to resolve, making substantial international treaties essential to adapt to rapid technological changes.

Technological progress in clean energy, climate modelling, and ecological capturing and exploration can also help approach climate change and other significant problems. Creating and spreading green technologies that can confront climate change and sustainable development are essential, showcasing technology's powerful and positive impact on humanity's well-being.

Reflecting on the impacts and implications requires deep consideration as the globe enters an era of unparalleled technological advancement. Balancing technology for societal betterment and reducing risks requires complex policies and planning. At this transformative turning point, more than ever, it takes the ongoing collaboration and shared vision of everyone to help utilise the benefits of technology for change around the world.

Environmental Considerations in Geopolitical Planning

The combination of environmental factors and geopolitical considerations has become increasingly urgent in discussions within society today. The relationships between nations or states, and other political or commercial divisions across the world, are significantly influenced by climate change, resource depletion, and ecological degradation. Rapid changes in the world's climate call for nations to urgently alter their climate policies to harness new opportunities and cope with the challenges that emerge from it.

The role of the environment in global dynamics, such as security, economic growth, international relations, and diplomatic ties with others, is critical. Climate change must be tackled alongside the increasing threats posed by natural disasters and rising sea levels to vulnerable populations, population centres, and critical infrastructure. Competition for fresh water and arable land fuels more conflicts and underscores stress on political relationships. Reduced resources mean increased tensions and confrontations, highlighting security issues.

In the context of diplomacy, the environment has served as one of the most important areas of cooperation and conflict between countries. The introduction of international treaties for climate change control, such as the Paris Agreement, underscores the importance of diplomacy in facilitating mitigation actions to reduce environmental perils. Equally, the efforts to achieve sustainable development targets alongside other conservation projects have generated cooperative activities that cut across political divides, thus illustrating the capacity of environmental matters to enhance international relations and shared governance.

From a strategic point of view, environmental processes warrant consideration in the design of geopolitical strategies to plan for and effectively deal with confronting situations. Climate and geography-defining positions and vulnerabilities are becoming increasingly important in national security doctrines for many geopolitical actors, necessitating the strengthening of climate and disaster resilience. Additionally, the development of new forms of renewable and environmentally friendly technologies has changed the concepts of energy security, thereby altering geo-strategic relationships and trade relations.

Different strategies must be adopted regarding the proactive and anticipatory aspects of environmental geopolitics to steer clear of predicaments. A clear understanding of environmental geopolitics demands blending environmental data with strategic planning, thereby providing an understanding of the changing geopolitical environment that considers all developed factors. With these considerations, policies and strategies can be developed to achieve international collaboration, strengthen adaptability, and develop sustainability for resources at a time overwhelmed by environmental challenges.

International Relations and Diplomatic Initiatives

The importance of diplomatic initiatives in international relations has often been understated. Statecraft operates on diplomacy, which enables countries to communicate with one another and resolve concerns proactively for mutual benefit. Herein, we discuss the intricacies of diplomatic initiatives and their relevance in international relations.

At its most fundamental level, diplomacy encompasses negotiation, compromise, and conciliation. It enables governments to manage conflict and foster cooperation on various issues, from settling trade deals and security agreements to climate change and humanitarian aid. To be productive in diplomacy, a practitioner must possess excellent negotiation skills, cultural sensitivity, and an understanding of the historical and geopolitical milieu that each bilateral or multilateral relationship involves.

Furthermore, diplomacy is significant in assisting with the complex maze of international organisations and forums. The United Nations, the World Trade Organisation, and even regional blocs like the European Union and ASEAN are platforms where states can engage in dialogue, forge relationships, and build normative frameworks for global governance. Through effective diplomacy, nations can utilise such institutions to promote their interests, defend international law, and participate in global decision-making.

Additionally, the functions of diplomatic missions and emissaries are quite important. Diplomats and ambassadors act as the essential link in the contacts between states, serving as agents of their governments and fostering understanding and trust. Knowledge of protocol, language, and local customs helps them facilitate the exchange of information, negotiate treaties, and settle conflicts. These diplomats further develop the relations of so-called "people to people" as well as culture on a wider scale, which extends beyond official diplomacy

In the contemporary global context, one cannot overlook the role of digital diplomacy as an important aspect of international relations. With the help of social networking sites, virtual meetings, and other online forums, governments practice public diplomacy by influencing public views, advancing policies, and establishing relations across borders. Digital technologies make it possible for leaders and citizens to interact directly and respond quickly to world happenings and emergencies, therefore stretching the hands and impact of diplomacy.

In concluding the aforementioned, achieving any diplomatic activity hinges on inclusivity and mutual respect. The roots of embracing diversity and recognising all sovereign states as equal while not interfering with the dictates of any country remain guiding principles of diplomacy. Thus, the sustenance of diplomacy can enable trust and collaboration to help construct sustainable peace, enhance economic development, and reduce the chances of conflict in a world of interdependence.

Multilateral Organisations' Role in Shaping the Future

The development of global stability and cooperation relies heavily on multilateral organisations, like the United Nations, European Union, and World Trade Organisation, which serve as avenues for diplomatic activities and relationships between various countries. They establish norms, solve conflicts, and encourage greater sustainable development goals and economic integration of nations. These bodies, through multilateral means, have the capacity to resolve many pressing international issues, and their development plays a tremendous impact on relations, both inter-country dependency and the balance of power across the globe. In this era of increased globalisation, their influence becomes more important.

Multilateral organisations have the potential to significantly promote dialogue and negotiation for the member states. They provide a neutral forum for debating and are effective in the elimination of block politics at international cooperation. They facilitate joint and bottom-up solutions to issues and solutions that not only help in reaching consensus but also help in understanding the complex issues. International Law and other human rights issues have single multi-purpose systems having universal jurisdiction and other basic laws where these bodies help in bringing integration.

They help build a more just and secure world by providing platforms for discussing and reaching agreements on humanitarian assistance, climate change, and disarmament.

Besides dealing with world politics, the scope of activities of multilateral organisations also includes coordinating economic activities, trade, public health, culture, and a range of other spheres. By coordinating policies and common standards, they promote conditions for profitable cooperation between countries. Indeed, these organisations also play an indispensable role in dealing with supranational issues such as pandemics, environmental issues, and migration crises, which no nation can properly address alone.

Multilateral organisations are also vital in responding to the most recent changes in technology and newly emerging geopolitical realities. They serve as discussion platforms on disruptive technologies, cybersecurity, and the use of innovations for purposes other than intended. They aid in formulating policies/standards and control international relations by using such technologies. Thus, multilateral organisations render decisions to influence the future technological environment for democracy, transparency, and observance of human rights.

In summary, prompt action and active cooperation of multilateral organisations are necessary to strengthen the position for enduring global peace and sustainable development.

Those functions are essential for fostering a future with sustained forward movement (progress), resilience, and inclusivity while adapting to emerging needs.

Closing Thoughts: Charting a Course for Global Stability

As we wrap up this particular scrutiny of proposed scenarios for tackling global politics in the foreseeable future, we need to equally emphasise the focus on achieving stable global order targets. The sheer pace of change in international relations requires a proactive response to the new interplay of factors and relations shaping the present geopolitical environment.

A stable global order relies heavily on several complex issues, such as economic strength, cooperation in providing security, technological advances, and responsible environmental policies. Balancing competing national priorities offers a much harsher challenge for promoting sensible policies that can openly present the myriad of opportunities or solve the problems imposed by pluralistic national interests and multilateral institutions that function on consensus.

Maintaining global stability hinges on understanding interdependence and interconnectedness. Diplomacy should take a more proactive and integrative approach beyond mere power politics and foster an atmosphere that encourages understanding and peaceful coexistence.

Mutual cooperation strengthens strategic culture, which can reduce the risk of power competition and increase a region's stability.

In addition, understanding the other side of global stability entails appreciating new technologies. Innovating creates new ethical and security issues, but innovation is essential for progress that is beneficial to people. Researching and developing new technologies to help society is just as important as protecting the natural world because environmental preservation contributes to lasting global stability.

Defining the reasons for global stability entails that international actors globally should respect the values inherent to an international order that abides by laws. This strengthens respect for human rights, democracy, and fighting international crime. Meeting those conditions improves the possibility of neutralising negative impacts and increases peace and stability in all countries.

When we speak of achieving global stability, it becomes apparent that actions must be taken with innovative thinking and flexibility in mind. In simpler terms, it requires a balanced commitment to international cooperation for objectives greater than self-centred goals. In dealing with the unknown issues presented in the 21st century, we are driven towards purely stable environments where eradicating violence must be prioritised so that a peaceful and prosperous future can be built.

Selected Bibliography

Books

1. Allison, G. (2017). *Destined for war: Can America and China escape Thucydides's trap?* Houghton Mifflin Harcourt.

2. Beeson, M. (2018). *China's rise and regional integration in East Asia: Hegemony or community?* Palgrave Macmillan.

3. Blanchard, J. M. F. (2019). *China's Maritime Disputes*. Rowman & Littlefield.

4. Bracken, P. (2016). *The second nuclear age: Strategy, danger, and the new power politics*. St. Martin's Press.

5. Brooks, R., & Wohlforth, W. C. (2016). *America abroad: The United States' global role in the 21st century*. Oxford University Press.

6. Buckley, C. (2020). *China's "Ukraine"? The Sino-Indian border crisis*. Yale University Press.

7. Buzan, B. (2014). *An introduction to the English School of International Relations: After forty years*. Polity Press.

8. Christensen, T. J. (2015). *The China challenge: Shaping the choices of a rising power*. W.W. Norton & Company.

9. Clarke, M. (2017). *China's capitalist revolution: The inside story of reform*. Palgrave Macmillan.

10. Friedberg, A. L. (2011). *A contest for supremacy: China, America, and the struggle for mastery in Asia*. W.W. Norton & Company.

11. Gagnon, J. P. (2019). *China's quest for Asia: Strategic implications of Beijing's new activism*. Palgrave Macmillan.

12. Godement, F. (2017). *China at sea: An ambitious maritime power*. European Council on Foreign Relations.

13. Goldstein, A. (2019). *Peak China: The rise and fall of the Chinese economy*. University of California Press.

14. Ikenberry, G. J. (2018). *The end of the American

century*. Polity Press.

15. Jacques, M. (2012). *When China rules the world: The end of the western world and the birth of a new global order*. Penguin Books.

16. Johnston, A. I. (2019). *Engaging China: Myth, aspiration, and reality*. Harvard University Press.

17. Kang, D. C. (2010). *East Asia before the West: Five centuries of trade and tribute*. Columbia University Press.

18. Kissinger, H. (2011). *On China*. Penguin Books.

19. Kurlantzick, J. (2016). *State capitalism: How the return of statism is transforming the world*. Oxford University Press.

20. Layne, C. (2012). *The Peace of Illusions: American Grand Strategy from 1940 to the Present*. Cornell University Press.

21. Liff, A. P. (2020). *China's military modernization: New capabilities and strategies for America's rapid-paced competitor*. Georgetown University Press.

22. Mearsheimer, J. J. (2014). *The tragedy of great power politics*. W.W. Norton & Company.

23. Nathan, A. J., & Scobell, A. (2012). *China's search

for security*. Columbia University Press.

24. Nye, J. S. (2015). *Is the American Century Over?* Polity Press.

25. Pillsbury, M. (2015). *The hundred-year marathon: China's secret strategy to replace America as the global superpower*. Henry Holt and Co.

26. Shambaugh, D. (2020). *China's leader: Assessing Xi Jinping's leadership*. Polity Press.

27. Shen, W. (2019). *The Rise of China and the Chinese World Order*. University of Michigan Press.

28. Swaine, M. D. (2015). *Confidence- and security-building measures in the new Taiwan Strait*. Carnegie Endowment for International Peace.

29. Tellis, A. J., & Tanner, J. (2020). *Strategic Asia 2020: 20 years of strategic review*. National Bureau of Asian Research.

30. Wang, J. (2016). *China's search for global order: From peace to harmonious world*. Palgrave Macmillan.

31. Wasserstrom, J. N. (2018). *Vigil: Hong Kong on the Brink*. Columbia Global Reports.

32. Weitz, R. (2017). *China-Russia relations*. Rowman & Littlefield.

33. Yahuda, M. (2013). *China's role in world affairs*. Routledge.

34. Yuan, J. (2015). *China and International Relations: The Chinese View and the Contribution of Wang Gungwu*. Palgrave Macmillan.

35. Zhang, Y. (2019). *China's Military Modernization: Implications for the United States*. Routledge.

Journal Articles and Book Chapters

- A. Rashid & Amir Ahmed Khuhro. (2023). *Historical insights of global power transitions: Implications on US-China relations*. Perennial journal of history, 4(2), 68-87. https://doi.org/10.52700/pjh.v4i2.156

- Ahmed Bux Jamali, Mehmood Hussain, & Hongsong Liu. (2024). *US-China competition*. In collection (pp. 276-290). https://doi.org/10.4324/9781003439110-23

- Alessandro Brambilla. (2017). *Graham Allison - Destined for war. Can America and China escape Thucydides's trap?*

- Alexandr Shalak. (2021). *American-Chinese confrontation from the perspective of Thucydides trap.* Journal of Political Science, 5(2), 110-118. https://doi.org/10.17150/2587-7445.2021.5(2).110-118

- Analysis of the US-China rivalry within the framework of the Thucydides trap: a theoretical analysis. (2023). Akademik Hassasiyetler, 10(21), 459-481. https://doi.org/10.58884/akademik-hassasiyetler.1257645

- Andrew R. Novo. (2016). *Where we get Thucydides wrong: The fallacies of history's first "hegemonic" war.* Diplomacy & Statecraft, 27(1), 1-21. https://doi.org/10.1080/09592296.2016.1137730

- Andrew Scobell. (2022). *Thucydides's trap? Historical interpretation, logic of inquiry, and the future of Sino-american relations.* Political Science Quarterly, 137(2), 405-406. https://doi.org/10.1002/polq.13307

- Arunesh Goswami. (2022). *Balancing grand strategy for America to offset Thucydides's trap with China.* Journal of Strategic Security, 15(2), 17-33. https://doi.org/10.5038/1944-0472.15.2.1983

- Atindra Dahal. (2020). *An assessment on genesis and justifiability of Thucydides trap on pretext of Asian century & China's charismatic rise.*

- Barbara Lippert & Volker Perthes. (2020). *Strategic*

rivalry between United States and China: causes, trajectories, and implications for Europe.

- Biao Zhang. (2019). *The perils of hubris? A tragic reading of "Thucydides' trap" and China-US relations*. Journal of Chinese Political Science, 24(1), 129-144. https://doi.org/10.1007/S11366-019-09608-Z

- Brandon K. Yoder. (2019). *Uncertainty, shifting power and credible signals in US-China relations: Why the "Thucydides trap" is real, but limited*. Journal of Chinese Political Science, 24(1), 87-104. https://doi.org/10.1007/S11366-019-09606-1

- Brian Cook. (2025). *Systemic wisdom and complex strategic competition: a systems approach*. SN Social Sciences, 5(2). https://doi.org/10.1007/s43545-024-01041-1

- C. Fred Bergsten. (2018). *China and the United States: the contest for global economic leadership*. China & World Economy, 26(5), 12-37. https://doi.org/10.1111/CWE.12254

- Carlos Aguiar de Medeiros & Nicholas Trebat. (2024). *From complementarity to rivalry: The political economy of United States-China relations*. Journal of Economic Issues, 58(2), 525-532. https://doi.org/10.1080/00213624.2024.2344431

- Carsten Rauch. (2017). *A tale of two power transi-*

tions: Capabilities, satisfaction, and the will to power in the relations between the United Kingdom, the United States, and Imperial Germany. International Area Studies Review, 20(3), 201-222. https://doi.org/10.1177/2233865916689510

- Chunman Zhang & Xiaoyu Pu. (2019). *Introduction: Can America and China escape the Thucydides trap?*. Journal of Chinese Political Science, 24(1), 1-9. https://doi.org/10.1007/S11366-019-09609-Y

- Ciwan Maksut Can & Anson K.C. Chan. (2022). *Preventive or revisionist challenge during power transition? The case of China–USA strategic competition.* The Journal of Asian Security & International Affairs, 9(1), 7-25. https://doi.org/10.1177/23477970221076646

- Daniel J. Lynch. (2019). *Destined for war: Can America and China escape Thucydides's trap?*. History: Reviews of New Books, 47(6), 164-166. https://doi.org/10.1080/03612759.2019.1661705

- David C. Kang & Xinru Ma. (2018). *Power transitions: Thucydides didn't live in East Asia.* Washington Quarterly, 41(1), 137-154. https://doi.org/10.1080/0163660X.2018.1445905

- Dmitry V. Yefremenko. (2020). *A double Thucydides trap: Donald Trump's presidency and new bipolarity.* Russia in Global Affairs, 18(3), 76-97. https://doi.org/10.31278/1810-6374-2020-18-3-76-97

- Duong Tuan Anh. (2022). *Geopolitics, the Thucydides trap, and the China–Pakistan–India trilateral.* In collection (pp. 128-141). https://doi.org/10.4324/9781003250920-10

- Edmund Li Sheng. (2023). *U.S.–China relations in Donald Trump's administration: The Belt and Road Initiative and the Thucydides trap.* In collection (pp. 35-59). https://doi.org/10.1007/978-981-99-7865-6_2

- Enescan Lorci. (2024). *Thucydides trap revisited.* Perspectives on Global Development and Technology, 22(3-4), 190-216. https://doi.org/10.1163/15691497-12341658

- Falin Zhang. (2021). *Power contention and international insecurity: A Thucydides trap in China–US financial relations?* Journal of Contemporary China, 30(131), 751-768. https://doi.org/10.1080/10670564.2021.1889229

- Gabriel Esteban Merino. (2024). *China and US systemic rivalry in the contemporary transition of world power.* In collection (pp. 54-72). https://doi.org/10.4324/9781032664941-4

- George Tridimas. (2024). *The political economy of the original "Thucydides' trap": A conflict economics perspective on the Peloponnesian war.* Public Choice. https://doi.org/10.1007/s11127-024-01179-9

- Graham Allison. (2017). *Destined for war: Can America and China escape Thucydides's trap?* Houghton Mifflin Harcourt.

- Gregory J. Moore. (2017). *Avoiding a Thucydides trap in sino-american relations (...and 7 reasons why that might be difficult)*. Asian Security, 13(2), 98-115. https://doi.org/10.1080/14799855.2017.1286162

- Hongtao Li. (2023). *The hegemonic rivalry between the United States and the People's Republic of China: European Union's place*. Advanced sciences and technologies for security applications, 3-46. https://doi.org/10.1007/978-3-031-28336-9_2

- Huan Yang. (2022). *Thucydides in China*. KNOW: A Journal on the Formation of Knowledge, 6(2), 351-371. https://doi.org/10.1086/721421

- Imad A. Moosa. (2020). *The Thucydides trap as an alternative explanation for the US–China trade war*. Global Journal of Emerging Market Economies, 12(1), 42-55. https://doi.org/10.1177/0974910119896644

- Ijaz Khalid. (2022). *Major powers rivalries: Analysis of war (choice or compulsion)*. Global strategic & security studies review, VII(IV), 8-16. https://doi.org/10.31703/gsssr.2022(vii-iv).02

- James C. MacDougall. (2017). *Destined

for war: Can America and China escape Thucydides's trap? Parameters, 47(2), 1-12. https://press.armywarcollege.edu/cgi/viewcontent.cgi?article=2937&context=parameters

- James Lee. (2019). *Did Thucydides believe in Thucydides' trap? The history of the Peloponnesian war and its relevance to U.S.-China relations.* Journal of Chinese Political Science, 24(1), 67-86. https://doi.org/10.1007/S11366-019-09607-0

- Jonathan Kirshner. (2019). *Offensive realism, Thucydides traps, and the tragedy of unforced errors: Classical realism and US-China relations.* 1(1), 51-63. https://doi.org/10.1007/S42533-019-00013-Y

- Jyotishman Bhagawati. (2017). *Destined for war: Can America and China escape Thucydides's trap?* Maritime Affairs: Journal of The National Maritime Foundation of India, 9, 95-97. https://doi.org/10.1080/09733159.2017.1412578

- L. Estachy. (2020). *Power struggle between China and the United States: Lessons of history.* 13(1), 82-99. https://doi.org/10.24833/2071-8160-2020-1-70-82-99

- Lam Peng Er. (2016). *China, the United States, alliances, and war: Avoiding the Thucydides trap?* Asian Affairs: An American Review, 43(2), 36-46. https://doi.org/10.1080/00927678.2016.1150765

- Lawrence Freedman. (2017). *Destined for war: Can*

America and China escape Thucydides's trap? Prism: A Journal of the Center for Complex Operations, 7(1), 1-12. https://doi.org/10.1111/NPQU.11444

- Lidan Ma. (2020). *Ways for China to solve Thucydides trap in the perspective of globalization.* In Proceedings (pp. 394-397). https://doi.org/10.2991/ASSEHR.K.200316.088

- Lyle J. Goldstein. (2015). *Meeting China halfway: How to defuse the emerging US-China rivalry.*

-Magí Castelltort Claramunt. (2021). *El posible conflicto bélico entre Estados Unidos y China: reconsiderando la «Trampa de Tucídides».* 17, 271-300.

- Mario Maritan. (2023). *The anti-China bias and why Thucydides trap is just an invention (and a dangerous one).* 37.

- Mario Maritan. (2024). *US imperialism and its legacies in East Asia: Thucydides Trap or Thrasymachus Paradox?* Fudan Journal of the Humanities and Social Sciences. https://doi.org/10.1007/s40647-024-00402-7

- Melissa Hamilton & Mark Fisher. (2024). *Opening the Thucydides trap: a genealogy of rise-and-fall theory.* International Affairs, 100(3), 1189-1206. https://doi.org/10.1093/ia/iiae082

- Michael A. Peters et al. (2020). *US–China rivalry and 'Thucydides' trap': Why this is a misleading ac-

count. Educational Philosophy and Theory, 1-12. https://doi.org/10.1080/00131857.2020.1799739

- Min Hyung Kim. (2019). *A real driver of US-China trade conflict: The Sino-US competition for global hegemony and its implications for the future.* International Trade, 3(1), 30-40. https://doi.org/10.1108/ITPD-02-2019-003

- Min Ye. (2024). *Security in context (SiC): A novel theoretical and empirical approach to the US-China rivalry.* Review of Social Economy. https://doi.org/10.1080/00346764.2024.2312414

- Nasai Muhammad Gwadabe. (2021). *The declining hegemony of the United States and the growing influence of China: A critical perspective on power transition theory in the 21st century.* Austral: Brazilian Journal of Strategy and International Relations, 9(18), 9-21. https://doi.org/10.22456/2238-6912.102434

- Oriana Skylar Mastro. (2019). *In the shadow of the Thucydides Trap: International relations theory and the prospects for peace in U.S.-China relations.* Journal of Chinese Political Science, 24(1), 25-45. https://doi.org/10.1007/S11366-018-9581-4

- Peter Hays Gries & Yiming Jing. (2019). *Are the US and China fated to fight? How narratives of 'power transition' shape great power war or peace.* Cambridge Review of International Affairs, 32(4),

456-482. https://doi.org/10.1080/09557571.2019.1623170

- Richard Ned Lebow & Feng Zhang. (2020). *Taming Sino-American rivalry.* Houghton Mifflin.

- Sam Bateman. (2016). *Meeting China halfway - How to defuse the emerging US-China rivalry.* Contemporary Southeast Asia: A Journal of International and Strategic Affairs, 38(2), 327-329. https://doi.org/10.1355/CS38-2L

- Sergio Gabriel Eissa. (2024). *Confucius' trap?* Perspectivas revista de ciencias sociales. https://doi.org/10.35305/prcs.v9i17.768

- Stefan Legge & Tomas Casas i Klett. (2020). *Thucydides Trap in the Business World: Corporate Strategy for a New Geopolitical Reality.* Social Science Research Network. https://doi.org/10.2139/SSRN.3563834

- Steve Chan. (2019). *More than one trap: Problematic interpretations and overlooked lessons from Thucydides.* Journal of Chinese Political Science, 24(1), 11-24. https://doi.org/10.1007/S11366-018-9583-2

- Ulrich Blum. (2023). *Chinas und Amerikas geoökonomische Rivalität: Gibt es die Gefahr einer Thukydides-Falle?* Wirtschaftsdienst, 103(3), 170-173. https://doi.org/10.2478/wd-2023-0048

- Valeri Modebadze. (2020). *US-China rivalry for*

global hegemony. Journal of Liberty and International Affairs, 6(2), 167-173. https://doi.org/10.47305/JLIA2020167M

- William Ziyuan Wang. (2019). *Destined for misperception? Status dilemma and the early origin of US-China antagonism.* Journal of Chinese Political Science, 24(1), 49-65. https://doi.org/10.1007/S11366-018-09596-6

- Xiyu Lu. (2024). *Analysis of strategic competition between China and the United States in the New Cold War Era.* Advances in Economics, Management and Political Sciences, 124(1), 93-100. https://doi.org/10.54254/2754-1169/2024.17733

- Yixuan Wang. (2023). *Understanding the current China-US relationship through the "Thucydides Trap".* Journal of Student Research, 12(3). https://doi.org/10.47611/jsrhs.v12i3.4335

- Zbigniew Brzezinski. (2014). *Can China avoid the Thucydides trap?* New Perspectives Quarterly, 31(2), 31-33. https://doi.org/10.1111/NPQU.11444

- Zhao Suisheng & Dan Guo. (2019). *A new cold war? Causes and future of the emerging US-China rivalry.* 19(1), 9-21. https://doi.org/10.22363/2313-0660-2019-19-1-9-21

- Zhaoying Han, Richard J. Cook, & Maximilian Ohle. (2019). *The Thucydides trap and the Kore-*

an peninsula: So why won't the USA and China get caught? Journal of Chinese Political Science, 24(1), 105-127. https://doi.org/10.1007/S11366-018-09595-7

- Zhou Meng. (2014). *China and the United States to avoid "Thucydides Trap": Realistic basis and approaches.* Journal of Fuyang Teachers College.

- Владимир Трапара. (2024). *The inverse Thucydides's trap: The structure and process of the US-China rivalry.* Međunarodni problemi, 76(2), 201-222. https://doi.org/10.2298/medjp2402201t

www.ingramcontent.com/pod-product-compliance
Lightning Source LLC
Chambersburg PA
CBHW031147020426
42333CB00013B/555